PRAISE FOR
TENDING GRIEF

"Camille Sapara Barton is a gift to all of us, because they understand that every single one of us will grieve, and they have given us a way to understand how we can grieve in community and center care in the inevitable transitions of our lives. This is what emergent strategy looks like at the precipice."

—ADRIENNE MAREE BROWN, author of
Pleasure Activism

"Camille Sapara Barton is undoubtedly one of our generation's luminaries, as this offering makes crystal clear. Camille's capacity to bring forward an imaginative yet consistently grounded and honest perspective about life's biggest inquiries—love, liberation, and loss—has made them a powerful and piercing voice in the emerging psychedelic ecosystem. It can be challenging to balance the visionary and the practical, made harder in a world that perpetually attempts to flatten and reduce everything holy to something consumable. Camille invites us all back into balance with the grace of a teacher and the patience of a parent, gently waiting for the rest of us to catch up."

—ISMAIL ALI, Policy and Advocacy Director
at the Multidisciplinary Association of
Psychedelic Studies (MAPS)

"In this beautiful little book, Camille Sapara Barton offers readers a powerful medicine, not only for being with and moving through grief, but for responding to the social injustice that sickens our world. Setting sharp, lucid political analysis alongside transformative somatic practices, *Tending Grief* is an essential map for anyone who longs for collective healing. This is an invaluable resource for changemakers everywhere."

—KAI CHENG THOM, author, mediator,
and somatic coach

"*Tending Grief* is a cauldron containing the right ingredients to center our individual and collective grief. The kind of grief and loss that makes us raw, come undone, unravel, and come into our humanness. The ingredients in this magical cauldron in the form of a book are the historical and ancestral understanding of how we hold grief in our bones and bring it into our movements. *Tending Grief* calls us to turn toward our grief, acknowledge and respond to it, and allow it to move through and change us. This book is a vital tool and resource for the times we are wading through, times that are mirroring to us the patterns of what must change and change now."

—MICHELLE C. JOHNSON, author of
Finding Refuge and *We Heal Together*

TENDING GRIEF

TENDING GRIEF

Embodied Rituals for Holding
Our Sorrow and Growing Cultures
of Care in Community

CAMILLE SAPARA BARTON

North Atlantic Books
Huichin, unceded Ohlone land
Berkeley, California

The Global Environments Network commissioned *The GEN Grief Toolkit*.

Published by	Cover art © cienpies via Getty Images
North Atlantic Books	Cover design by Jess Morphew
Huichin, unceded Ohlone land	Book design by Happenstance Type-O-Rama
Berkeley, California	

Printed in the United States of America

Tending Grief: Embodied Rituals for Holding Our Sorrow and Growing Cultures of Care in Community is sponsored and published by North Atlantic Books, an educational nonprofit based in the unceded Ohlone land Huichin (Berkeley, CA) that collaborates with partners to develop cross-cultural perspectives; nurture holistic views of art, science, the humanities, and healing; and seed personal and global transformation by publishing work on the relationship of body, spirit, and nature.

North Atlantic Books' publications are distributed to the US trade and internationally by Penguin Random House Publisher Services. For further information, visit our website at www.northatlanticbooks.com.

Library of Congress Cataloging-in-Publication Data

Names: Sapara Barton, Camille, 1991- author.
Title: Tending grief : embodied rituals for holding our sorrow and growing
    cultures of care in community / Camille Sapara Barton.
Description: Berkeley, California : North Atlantic Books, [2024] | Includes
    bibliographical references. | Summary: "An embodied guide to being with
    grief individually and in community-practical exercises, decolonized
    rituals, and Earth-based medicines for healing and processing loss"--
    Provided by publisher.
Identifiers: LCCN 2023033282 (print) | LCCN 2023033283 (ebook) | ISBN
    9781623179946 (paperback) | ISBN 9781623179953 (epub)
Subjects: LCSH: Grief--Social aspects. | Grief--Psychological aspects.
Classification: LCC BF575.G7 S2745 2024 (print) | LCC BF575.G7 (ebook) |
    DDC 152.4--dc23/eng/20231204
LC record available at https://lccn.loc.gov/2023033282
LC ebook record available at https://lccn.loc.gov/2023033283

1 2 3 4 5 6 7 8 9 KPC 28 27 26 25 24

This book is dedicated to Ayo, Oscar, and Gabi.

*Ayo, thank you for teaching me about
love, loss, and tending grief.*

*Oscar and Gabi, thank you for helping me to
integrate, shape shift, and move towards aliveness.*

CONTENTS

ACKNOWLEDGMENTS

This book would not exist without the guidance of my ancestors; thank you for opening the way. I am grateful for the plants, the mycelia, and the land(s) that have shaped me, that hold me in times of celebration and sorrow. To my mother, thank you for teaching me to follow my gut and embrace being a weirdo, dancing to the drum of my intuition. Thank you to my Nanna—the matriarch of the family—for your care and the life lessons. My writing process was supported by the kind eyes and feedback of Dre, Victoria, Theresa, Farzana, and Sanah—thank you for your friendship. I appreciate my family, blood and chosen, for all the love and the learning—I am because you are. Thank you Simon for your sunshine; your love and care are a deep blessing. Gratitude to Yvonne, for supporting my energy to flow with enough confidence to complete this. Thank you, Erwin, for reconnecting me to ancestral wisdom.

Many thanks to Nessie, Samirah, Simran, and the Global Environments Network (GEN) for helping me to birth *The GEN Grief Toolkit,* the foundation this book emerged from. To Mayis and Euphemia, thank you for planting the seeds that led me to dream of this research becoming a book. Finally, thank you to Gillian, Rebecca, and the team at North Atlantic Books for your care and support with this project—it is such a joy to feel in alignment with you.

INTRODUCTION

Welcome. Thank you for picking up this book and being curious about tending grief. It feels long overdue that we begin to reckon with and relearn how to hold the grief that ripples through and between us. The beloved abolitionist organizer Mariame Kaba puts it like this:

> As a society, we have long turned away from any social concern that overwhelms us. Whether it's war, climate change, or the prison-industrial complex, Americans have been conditioned to simply look away from profound harms. Years of this practice have now left us with endless wars, dying oceans, and millions of people in bondage and oppressively policed. It is time for a thorough, unflinching exam-ination of what our society has wrought and what we have become. It is time to envision and create alternatives to the hellish conditions our society has brought into being.[1]

Turning away from the challenges that overwhelm us is not limited to the North American psyche, but it is a common tendency in the West and many other places in the world. Considering this, it feels important to note that grief tending enables us to feel more; to care about the world we inhabit. "Joy is not the opposite of grief. Grief is the opposite of indifference."[2]

For you to situate where this writing has emerged from, I will begin by sharing some of the conditions that have shaped how I move through the world.

I am a Black British, mixed heritage, queer, gender expansive, neuro-divergent being who is thirty-one years old at the time of writing. I have navigated the choppy waters of chronic illness for most of my life, but thankfully I'm healthier now than I can remember. I was raised in North London within a predominantly Black, lower-middle-class family, within a majority white, upper-middle-class neighborhood. My mother's people are Yoruba (Nigerian) and Guyanese. Other than my dad, I had minimal contact with the paternal side of my family—who are a combination of English, Irish, and Scottish—due to their fundamentalist Christian beliefs that led them to end contact with us during my early years.

My mother parented in a socially conscious way; she taught me to trust my gut, introduced me to Black history and musical traditions, as well as herbal medicine. A singer-songwriter at heart, my dad put aside his dreams to work in office jobs to keep a roof over our heads and food on the table, which led him to work abroad for a few years of my childhood. When my parents officially divorced when I was twelve, my brothers and I stayed living with my mother, who continued to provide all the emotional labor and domestic care that sustained us. She gave us a lot of love and did her best to create a nourishing home life, filled with beauty. My childhood was characterized by a rich mixture of music, home-cooked food, political debate, and some formative adverse childhood experiences. As a family, it has been challenging to navigate the UK mental health system and the harms that come with that.

I grew up within a specific esoteric worldview as both my parents followed the teachings and meditation practice of an Indian spiritual teacher and peace advocate. This gave me an early introduction to the power of the breath and turning attention inward, as well as an aversion to spiritual bypassing which has fuelled my commitment to social change work.

It was clear to me as a child that my family was in a financially precarious position compared to those I was living in proximity to. Economic scarcity showed up in various ways, but ultimately we always had enough. I started working part-time at fourteen so I could have some money for adventures, live music gigs, and things that interested me. Growing up, I never went hungry and always had a roof over my head, so I recognise the privilege in that. I went to a high-performing state school and learnt to speak and contort myself in ways that enabled me to survive the majority white spaces I was immersed in during my teenage years and through university. I obsessively devoured raves and nightlife every weekend to drink in enough pleasure to get through the following school week and distract myself from the grief lingering within me. Mental health challenges and heavy substance use were a part of my life at this time.

Dance, altered states of consciousness, friendship, political somatics, and escaping my environment have kept me alive through the harder moments of my life. As a young adult, my body and mind were shaped by the unceded land of the Ohlone people, in what is commonly known as the San Francisco Bay Area in California. While living in the Bay Area, I was introduced to queer femme–led radical Black organizing, healing justice, research in psychedelic therapy, alternative approaches to world building, and grief tending. I am grateful for all the gifts and learning that I've received from being in this community context.

I am committed to the lifelong process of repatterning[3] my relationship to the land and more-than-human kin so I can become a steward of the earth rather than someone simply extracting from ecosystems. Part of this process involves shifting my cosmology away from monotheistic, Western universalism towards worldviews rooted in the African diaspora and the precolonial practices of my ancestors. I live in the hopeful practice of becoming a good ancestor, supporting the web of life.

I write this book from a place of humble learning and experience, rather than from a place of expertise. I am in the process of tending grief and figuring out how to develop models that can work for myself as well as the communities I am entangled with. I have a lot to learn and intend to keep doing so throughout my life.

Thank you for joining me in this process of exploration. I invite you to gently embrace what aligns with you and to leave what does not resonate with your experience.

How This Book Came to Exist

The publication of this book marks the completion of a seven-year cycle for me—all the cells in my body have renewed since the moment I descended into the depths of grief for the first time.

In 2017, I went into a grief spiral after having an abortion. The experience was incredibly eye-opening for me. I was full of rage and sadness, and bewildered by the lack of support or public space to be with this experience which is incredibly common in the UK and many parts of the world. During this time of being submerged in grief, I became aware of how little space there is in our Western societies for anyone to process feelings that do not support productivity. I craved ritual and intentional time to be with my grief, learn from it, and compost it through my body. I felt a deep longing for my Yoruba, Guyanese, and Celtic ancestral practices that were violently hidden through the colonization, displacement, and assimilation of my family. In order to find a way through, I developed my own rituals and read a great deal about grief and how to tend to it. I created the holding that I needed. In the process of tending to my grief, a domino effect took place—previously dissociated memories from years of childhood sexual abuse began to resurface, which led to me having to rewrite the story of my childhood and learn how to find safety in my body. A lot was unearthed.

Out of necessity, I became determined to find practices that could allow me to alchemize my loss, to allow it to become a generative force in my life rather than something that would continue to numb or constrict me. This desire led to deep conversations with Nessie Reid at the Global Environments Network (GEN) about the importance of grief work within movements for social change. Over time and after many deep chats, Nessie sought funding and a clear project developed: I was asked to research embodied grief practices to create a toolkit that could be used by those engaged in work for environmental, social, and healing justice. The intention of this toolkit was to provide simple rituals that would allow people to connect to grief while staying resourced and aware of their embodied experience in order to prevent overwhelm.

I began the GEN Grief Toolkit project in January 2020. A few months later, the world changed overnight and we descended into a collective grief experience—the COVID-19 pandemic. I spent a year and a half, mostly alone, researching the tools, experimenting on myself, tending to grief in my life and the lives of those close to me, being immersed in it all.

During the summer of 2021, we held a small, residential retreat to practice the tools with a group of fifteen people in the UK. I facilitated alongside Farzana Khan, with support and space holding from Nessie Reid, Samirah Siddiqui, and Raju Rage. It was generative and showed that this approach could have resonance for other people. The toolkit was released in January 2022 as a resource online, under a Creative Commons license. At the time of this writing, it has been downloaded over one thousand times with incredibly positive feedback from people.

In the months that followed, I received many requests for physical copies including from my students at Ecologies of Transformation in Amsterdam.[4] That planted the seed to see if this could become a published book. Some conversations later, North Atlantic Books felt like the right home for this work.

Grief tending is not *the* answer to all our social challenges. To claim a singular answer would be foolish given the expansive complexity of our world. However, I do believe that tending grief, loss, and lament; reconnecting to these cycles of life, love, and death that are present in our waking days, is essential in order to come back into right relationship with the world we are a part of and the more-than-human kin we share our home with. My hope is that grief tending can provide a first step towards composting practices of domination to get back into right relationship or, as Robin Wall Kimmerer says, to restore:

Restoration offers concrete means by which humans can once again enter into a positive, creative relationship with the more-than-human world, meeting responsibilities that are simultaneously material and spiritual. It's not enough to grieve. It's not enough to just stop doing bad things.[5]

I hope that this book can support processes of reconnection, sensing, and feeling that can move us towards full aliveness and collaboration-filled, livable futures.

Lineage

This book rests upon the shoulders of many ancestors who have shared their deep wisdom in the service of healing and life-sustaining practices for the next seven generations to come.[6] I would like to begin by thanking my Yoruba, Guyanese, and Celtic ancestors who guide me every day and enable me to remember what has been lost. I will uplift and thank Malidoma and Sobonfu Somé for their profound influence upon grief work in the Western world. Gratitude to Francis Weller—a student of Sobonfu and Malidoma—who wrote *The Wild Edge of Sorrow,* a book that has been deeply instructive. A big thank you to Martín Prechtel, who shaped my understanding about the interconnections between grief and praise in his book *The Smell of Rain on Dust.* Healing justice, Black feminism, and disability justice are key areas of study within my life that shape my thinking and practices—thank you to all the authors, disabled folks, healers, and activists who have created the path and shown me how to find my place within it. Deep gratitude and thanks to one of my teachers, Nkem Ndefo, who created the *Resilience Toolkit*—the somatic approach which underpins the embodiment practices used within this book. I stand on the shoulders of leaders within the political somatics lineage, namely Staci Haines of generationFIVE and Generative Somatics, as well as Rae Johnson. Blessings and thanks to Tricia Hersey of the Nap Ministry, who consistently reminds me that rest is a liberatory practice, as well as something which supports grief work. I would like to thank Cindy Milstein, who edited *Rebellious Mourning,* for showing me that grief has always been part of social movements. Gratitude and deep appreciation to adrienne maree brown, who overflows with prophetic wisdom—her visionary offerings and world-making inspire me deeply. I am indebted to the work of Octavia Butler, who continues to expand my imagination. Thank you to Stephen Jenkinson, the author of *Die Wise,* who helped me understand my first experience of grief and created an opening which continues to ripple out. I am ever inspired by and grateful for the beauty of Black people and the African diaspora, from which I draw so much strength, creativity, and inspiration every day. May our pleasure and grief rituals continue to heal, deepen, and grow.

How to Engage with This Book

As you explore, I invite you to pause when you need to. To be gentle with yourself and take breaks as needed. As you read, I invite you to notice any sensations, contraction, expansion, or memories that arise in your body or mind.

The book has been written with the intention of being read from start to finish. However, please engage as feels best for you. You can read it from front to back or skip straight to the conversations, the rituals, or whatever suits your needs. My hope is that you can find support to tend your grief without becoming overwhelmed. To gently ease into it. Many of the rituals can be done in as little as twenty minutes. Let us reclaim our feelings, compost the numbness, and move towards full aliveness.

THE ONGOING GRIEF
OF COLONIZATION

The loss never stopped. With colonization came the apocalypse—our ancestors lost their language, rituals, bodily autonomy, plant teachers, mutual aid with more-than-human kin, and ways of knowing. A white god was imposed, leading to the fracturing of the embodied knowledge that our rituals and cosmology used to intricately connect us to the web of life and our ancestors. This wound, freshly open, was followed by hundreds of years of exploitation so great that it made life in foreign lands seem appealing, or the only option to those recently colonized. This was a transition into a strange, gray world. The loss of the sun, abundant melanin, and eyes filled with care and trust was a huge shock to bodies already in survival mode. We must remember that

> colonialism isn't simply the physical occupation of land. It's a process, an operation of power in which one cosmology is extinguished and replaced with another. In that replacement, one set of interpretations about humans' place in the universe is supplanted. Patterns of identity,

language, culture, work, relationship, territory, time, community and care are transformed.[1]

Although this is framed as the past within linear time, the legacies of these events continue to unfold to this day.

As professor and author Christina Sharpe reminds us, we are in the Wake, living in the aftershocks of enslavement and Empire that embedded dynamics of superiority and inferiority that many still navigate, duck, and dive between in order to live another day.[2] It is normalized hostility that allows Black children to be shot when ringing a doorbell or playing in a playground in the US, and it is our lack of care for African children that allows them to work in unsafe conditions to mine the minerals that power our smartphones.[3] We bear witness to aftershocks in England and Wales where many mental health wards are overwhelmingly filled with Black and global majority[4] bodies, despite us being a fraction of the population.[5]

We have felt the dehumanization, normalized suffering, and disposability that have been associated with melanated bodies within the global economic order for the last five centuries. Even those of us weighed and measured as exceptional or "one of the good ones" are not immune to this legacy. Respectability will not save us.

May this spell be broken and our bodies be held as sacred by all beings, looked upon with kind eyes and trust. May we once again feel beautifully intertwined in the web of life, weaving reciprocity as we dance, the sun caressing our faces. May we know that our lives hold deep value and that they are intricately connected to the ecosystems we are a part of. May we have the space to share our gifts and be resourced enough to experience ease, rest, and pleasure in our days. May we have the courage to tend to our wounds and move towards aliveness.

How can we break this spell, compost the path of domination we are unconsciously marching along? I do not claim to have the answers, but I sense that tending to grief is a crucial place to begin.

Tending to my grief enabled me to orient to and understand the power dynamics and histories I am entangled in that were keeping me separate from many of my kin. This unraveling began while I was employed as an education mentor at a restorative justice school in West Oakland, California, with students who had been impacted by incarceration, food insecurity, and the war on drugs. I quickly realized that my insulated upbringing meant that I could not relate to what they were experiencing; I could only humbly listen and follow their lead as to what support beyond academics could look like.

I was raised in North London, in a lower-middle-class, predominantly Black family, in a majority white neighborhood, which was less policed and surveilled as a result. This environment afforded me certain benefits that improved my quality of life—such as clean air, accessible produce, and the safety to experiment with altered states within people's homes—but ultimately it did not protect me or my family from the harmful aftershocks of colonization. To survive, I learnt to contort myself into shapes that were deemed obedient, or interesting enough, in order to avoid a lot of the psychological and physical violence that landed on the bodies of the Black kin around me who refused to play this game. At the time, the cruelty was harder for me to detect and acknowledge, dressed as it was in polite, leafy-green, English suburbia.

While living in West Oakland, it became possible for me to hold the complexity of my childhood years, with its entanglements of privilege, harm, and love, in its messy fullness for the first time. To behold the real-life impacts of militarized policing, youth incarceration, and the war on drugs tapped me into deep wells of rage, grief, and sorrow as my body witnessed the brutality and disposability that so many Black and global majority people are surviving, and the way it's breaking apart families and targeting children. I felt powerless to prevent what my students were experiencing, and any savior complex that drew me into this role was smothered by the cold reality of the situation.

11

However, in the space beyond my compulsion to prove my usefulness, to feel worthy of Black love, I found kinship—a deep knowing that despite the real differences of our experiences, we navigated shared dynamics in the aftershocks of colonization and its imposed hierarchies. Our shared ability to improvise, spark joy, side-step inequality through care, and embody playful survival strategies resonated with me. I learnt that the collective legacies we are entangled with often suffocate the agency we place upon the individual in the West.

In many ways, this time broke apart who I had been, but it created fertile soil that I could use to grow into the person I would like to be. It also helped me to notice and research more deeply the many parallels of inequality in the UK—including classism, ableism, racism within the policing and criminal justice system, food insecurity, and similar impacts to the Black community via the war on drugs. Before my time in the US, I had been under the illusion that the UK was somehow "better" than the US in terms of equality, but I came to see that it is simply a different flavor of the same dynamics (with the harm somewhat insulated by the UK's National Health Service [NHS] and social welfare system).[6]

The middle-class bubble I grew up in shielded me from what many working-class, Black and global majority folks were coming up against in London during the 90s. I grieved when I realized that such shielding operates to ensure that people who grew up in similar contexts to me would endorse certain positions on the chess board of society and reinforce the status quo, including the disposability of certain bodies to benefit the few. This sorrow inspired my curiosity about how I could interrupt this logic and learn to play a different game with the aim of reconnecting and growing solidarity with my Black and global majority kin as well as working-class people. I realized that the benefits of upward mobility for Black folks in the diaspora so often come with a severing from wider community networks and the *real safety* of kinship that exists within community care.

This experience allowed me to begin my ongoing journey of witnessing my conditioned tendencies[7] and following ancestral guidance to repair the connection to kin that was unconsciously sacrificed by my elders in order to move towards the promise of "success." I notice what has been integrated and what I still need to cultivate or repattern so I can move toward connection, shedding tendrils of superiority and perfectionism. I continue to learn, become, make mistakes, pick myself up again, and repair. This process is messy and perfectly imperfect, but undeniably bound with my heart, which continues to expand to love and feel sorrow in equal measure. As Martín Prechtel reminds us, love and grief are two sides of the same coin.[8]

In 2014, I had the pleasure of attending a day-long grief ritual with Sobonfu Somé in California. Sobonfu and Malidoma Somé are ancestors of the Dagara tribe, rooted in what is now known as Burkina Faso, who spent many years sharing the wisdom of the Dagara to support grief work and ritual transformation in the West. The grief ritual I attended with Sobonfu included drumming throughout and different altar spaces adorned and tenderly held by the community. During the process, people were invited to intuitively move between active grieving, ancestor veneration, drumming, and support of other community members. This flow allowed for an organic unfolding of grief, care, and community support. I am deeply indebted to their work; this book rests on their shoulders.

According to Sobonfu, the Dagara

> see that in life it is necessary to grieve those things that no longer serve us and let them go. When I grieve, I am surrounded by family reassuring me that the grieving is worthwhile and I can grieve as much as I want. We experience conflicts, loved ones die or suffer, dreams never manifest, illnesses occur, relationships break up, and there are unexpected natural disasters. It is so important to have ways to release those pains to keep clearing ourselves. Hanging on to old pain just makes it grow until it smothers our creativity, our joy, and our ability to connect with others. It may even kill us. Often my community uses grief rituals to heal wounds and open us to spirit's call.[9]

In Dagara communities, people are expected to express their grief in monthly group rituals. It is taboo to skip the monthly rites as unprocessed grief is believed to affect the community in a myriad of negative ways, becoming material harm in the form of violence or illness.

I believe in the effect of skipping this ritual. We need to tend our grief in order to expand our imaginations; however, we must first acknowledge the extraction and domination that has destroyed so many worlds in the last few hundred years of Empire and its aftershocks. Without feeling into our past, how possible is it to imagine new futures? Alternative worlds existed before the universalism of the West and the neoliberal logics that became bound with standard notions of time, which were imposed by the British to regulate the day around production. In *Capitalist Realism,* Mark Fisher argued that it is easier for most people to imagine the end of the world than the end of capitalism.[10] Perhaps we need some space to grieve this stolen imagination? This forgetting that other ways of living have existed and are possible? Perhaps spending curious moments with these traces of past realities can guide us towards livable futures?

What unfolds in the following pages is a cluster of noticing from my own life and from the lives of the kin around me, from the wisdom of my body and the bodies of my ancestors. I invite you to integrate what is nourishing to you and discard what does not align. I invite you to remember, to feel the grief that may linger within . . . the longing to light candles beside the pictures of dead loved ones and tell stories about them, or to be held with tenderness while you cry about a difficult ending, for your rage about precolonial worlds assimilated to be honored. As you meander, I invite you to notice the whispers that sing your part to play in livable futures to come, should you choose to hear them. Ultimately, as adrienne maree brown reminds us,

> we are living inside the imagination of people who thought economic disparity and environmental destruction were acceptable costs for their power. It is our right and responsibility to write ourselves into the future.

All organizing is science fiction. If you are shaping the future, you are a futurist. And visionary fiction is a way to practice the future in our minds, alone and together.[11]

The Past as Present

History is not the past, it is the present. We carry our history with us. We are our history.

—JAMES BALDWIN, in *I Am Not Your Negro: A Companion Edition to the Documentary Film Directed by Raoul Peck*

My ancestors have not had space to grieve their assimilation into the West and the hurts that have come with it. To get on with life, in the gray space with unkind eyes, they learnt to improvise through chaos and crisis, while supporting others in the midst of it all. Mutual aid in the form of a *susu,* or a box, as Guyanese folks call it, enabled many in my grandmother's generation to save money for bigger purchases, such as a deposit for a house, at a time when banks would not lend to Afro-Caribbean folks. Side-stepping inequality through care and support is what the Windrush generation learnt to do. The *Windrush generation* refers to predominantly Caribbean people who came to England from Commonwealth countries colonized by the British between 1948 and 1971. Some, but not all, arrived on HMT *Empire Windrush*—a ship that became a symbol of the mass migration that took place during this time. This generation was instrumental in rebuilding Britain after World War II. Many became health workers in the newly formed NHS and others worked in transport, manual labor, and domestic work. In many cases, they were invited to support the "motherland" only to discover, upon arrival, that they were not seen as British by those who benefitted from the Commonwealth. They were met with unkind eyes and a cascade of discrimination which viscerally showed exactly what the motherland thought of them. To make a life in the gray space, this community found that mutual aid was essential for survival.

In present time, for the descendants of the Windrush generation, caring for each other is still necessary to survive in our daily lives. Many Black women and queer elders have supported me while I navigated the hostile waters of exploitative, white-dominated academic institutions that are interested in gaining from the optics of our bodies with little regard for our mental health. Without trusted kin with kind eyes, I would not have made it through. I think of my family—one of many Black families navigating the UK mental health system with relatives diagnosed with schizophrenia, often after a cascade of traumatic events—the ways we reach out to community, how we ask for advice about which wards to avoid, which antipsychotics are bad news, and how to advocate for our relatives within the system. Perhaps we get a tip for a supportive and affordable lawyer who may be able to support us after an incident of police violence against our young relative who needs someone to stand up for them so that they know—this is not right. This is not how it is meant to be. Do you notice this side-stepping or dance around inequality in your life? Are there ways in which you and your trusted ones get together to create a soft(er) landing after rupture?

We grieve when we know that, currently, we ultimately cannot prevent the manifestations of inequality from arising; but we can create a space in which to breathe, recuperate, and find the strength to meet the next week. I learnt this from the Windrush, my grandmother's generation. They worked, laughed, resisted and refused, danced, grew culture, and celebrated the joy of being alive, even in adverse conditions. However, at times the honed skill of finding the silver lining would break apart, unleashing volcanic eruptions of rage, anxiety, or deep sadness. All a manifestation of the untapped wells of stress and grief buried beneath the surface. The volcano moments were never mentioned again after the lava had cooled. I once asked a beloved elder why they did not allow themself to cry freely, and they responded, "If I let myself cry, I am afraid I won't ever stop." The unspoken consensus among my elders growing up was that it's better to bottle up challenging emotions; keep it moving and be thankful for your blessings.

As an adult I have come to realize that tears are necessary. Grief is a vital antidote to the zombie-like state so many of us are inhabiting in the gray space, sacrificing our bodies to grind culture at the altar of modernity, anointing ourselves with the mantra: this is progress, this is the way to be successful.[12] We exhaust and break our bodies, chasing the golden carrot towards excessive wealth and material possessions, thinking these things are going to fulfill us. They won't. They provide temporary satisfaction before the empty (void) inside calls us to consume again.

Why do we consent to this extractive economic system, built off the backs of our ancestors and the earthly riches plundered from our home-lands? It's making us sick, but we don't see because we've trained ourselves not to feel. Colonization conditioned us to feel less, punished us for using our practices to connect to spirit or grief, or to our bodies and lands in ways Europeans deemed primitive. Now we struggle to move beyond the numbness of convenience. We have not shed tears for our homelands that continue to be raped and pillaged by foreign corporations under the guise of development as the profiteers loot to the mantra: *this is progress*. We have not acknowledged that we are heartbroken about the imposition of the gender binary, absent in many precolonial contexts within Africa until the invasion of Western powers, which in present time continue to incite state violence against LGBTQ+ Africans, for example in Uganda due to lobbying from US Christian organizations.[13] We have barely lamented the way our languages are disappearing within our ancestral lands, replaced by the one tongue, supposedly more valuable or "civilized."[14]

Perhaps this is why we still allow European colonial powers to control the education system in many of their former colonies? We have not mourned how much has been taken from us. We have forgotten how to speak with the trees or the birds. We are disconnected, often hungry for intimacy, vulnerability, and connection, but searching in all the wrong places. We bypass the fracturing to salivate over images of Black billionaires, convinced that if we *just* work harder, we can get a bigger slice of the pie and find the happiness we are told that monetary riches bring. As the impacts of climate change get louder, with poisoned soil and water ways crying out for care, many in the West ignore the fact that we cannot eat money.[15]

Making money by any means necessary is not a viable survival strategy. Many struggle as late-stage capitalism consumes melanated bodies in the so-called Global South to create convenience culture for a small percentage of the world. Even those of us living in the gated communities of the West may find that without economic systems change, our access to housing, food, and care will become precarious as we age. This system is consuming us for the benefit of an economic elite that does not care about most of us or the planet. Again, respectability will not lead us to liberation. As Audre Lorde reminds us, "The Master's tools will not dismantle the Master's House."[16]

So what does it look like to grow something new? To move away from this game of individualist hustle culture that is not only killing us, breaking our bodies, but also destroying our ecosystems? How long will we turn away from what is happening? What will we tell our grandchildren if they ask us why there is no clean water to drink or what we did while the soil was being poisoned? I doubt the explanation "If I wasn't doing it, someone else would have been" will feel satisfying.

We need to feel. To slow down and sense what is happening. To grieve and understand what has been lost so that we can begin to assess how to move in a different direction, not simply repeat the behaviors that have led us to this place. We need to interrupt the mindless extraction from our bodies and ableist constructions of productivity. We need to reconnect to our divinity. As Trisha Hersey reminds us, rest is resistance.[17] Our ancestors knew how to rest; they understood that our bodies are sacred, regardless of what we do or don't produce as workers. We need to reconnect with the wonder of this life and the ecosystems we belong to so that we can pause, slow down, and notice what we want to leave behind for future generations; what it means to be a good ancestor; and how we can practice this in our daily lives.

I sense that members of my generation are some of the first within the gray space that now have some of the tools, language, and spaciousness to tend to these wounds. To begin to notice them, to clean them out, and to apply soothing balms so they may begin to transform, repattern, or move towards collective healing. We are reconnecting with ancestral practices for grief or lament that were discarded or forgotten when we were assimilated into the West.

Before colonization, our ancestors had community-based rituals to process the grief of lost loved ones or ways of existing. Held space for grief in community is an act of deep care, an offering that sustains life by composting loss. These rituals provided our ancestors with a space to let go and surrender to feeling without having to be careful with language or responsible for holding it together. It was a space in which you could allow the wave of loss to flow through whilst you were being supported, without fear of being judged or having to suppress what you needed to release. I long for this space—I know it exists in between the cracks and can be remade within diaspora communities.

COVID-19 and the Aftershocks

Like Arundhati Roy, I see the pandemic as a portal, a seismic shift that changed life as we knew it overnight.[18] Another end of the world. As I write, we are three years into this journey of loss and uncertainty, still orienting to the moment we find ourselves in, surrounded by the debris of isolated companionship with algorithms and screens, a corrosive balm for loneliness. The virus is still rippling among us, pulsating alongside the push to "get back to normal." The neoliberal lullaby seeks to induce cognitive dissonance; however, many people, including disabled and chronically ill folks, are aware that this public health crisis is still present tense. Some prefer to forget.

To date, I have not witnessed any collective, state-initiated moments to honor the dead or reflect upon this collective trauma we have experienced and continue to experience. To do so in public space would jeopardize the needs of the market, so hungry for us all to become productive workers and consumers again. What is alive in the field is a growing awareness of trauma and an array of mostly individualized approaches to tend to this. I am curious about who these approaches serve? What story does this tell about the world and how we can live in a way that serves the web of life? I think there is much to learn from liberation psychology which seeks to address and acknowledge the environmental or systemic conditions that create harm in the collective, rather than pathologizing individuals.

In these sticky yet memorable years within the pandemic portal, I have been struck by how present the ongoing aftershocks of colonization are and have felt the waves of grief that come with this realization. This time has illuminated harmful inequalities that have been bubbling under the surface for decades; now clear for many to see. The veil is thin. Black and global majority communities in the UK, the US, and perhaps other nations have witnessed the bodies of our melanin-kissed kin perish at far higher rates than white people, despite us being a fraction of the population.[19] Along with the added weight of racialized police violence during this time, our bodies and communities are experiencing a great deal of grief.

In *Inflamed: Deep Medicine and the Anatomy of Injustice,* Rupa Marya and Raj Patel provide a map to help us understand how and why many Black and global majority communities in the UK and US have been disproportionately impacted by the virus.[20] Inflammation is the key—an embodied byproduct of inequality such as racialized harm, colonial domination, or displacement. Since the virus also causes inflammation, it has been more deadly to those inhabiting bodyminds that are already more inflamed due to historical and ongoing structural conditions.

Another important aspect is also exposure because many Black and global majority folks have been frontline workers during the pandemic. As of 2022, 25 percent of the National Health Service (NHS) workforce was made up of global majority workers.[21] One study looking at ethnic disparities between health and social care workers during the pandemic found "evidence of ethnic disparities across several workplace hazards, with increased exposure to and less protection against infection, more responsibility for the clinical management of infection, and evidence of systemic racial bias in the disproportionate redeployment of minority ethnic nursing staff to COVID-19 areas."[22] The politics of disposability are at play and the hangover of superiority stinks of colonial dynamics. Global majority folks were and continue to be overrepresented in other areas of frontline work—in transport, retail, and distribution.[23] This is mirrored in other Organization for Economic Co-operation and Development (OECD) countries too, including the United States.[24] Our kin is keeping society going yet receiving very little thanks in return—perhaps people clapped in the streets at the height of pandemic chaos, yet frontline workers have received no pay rise to meet inflation as the dust settles.

During the pandemic, many Black British people have been trying to recover from the Windrush scandal which, most visibly, took place from 2018 to 2020. This involved the UK government unlawfully classifying thousands of the Windrush generation as illegal immigrants despite them having been given indefinite right to remain when they arrived in the UK. The UK government destroyed their landing cards so there was no longer "evidence" of their arrival decades ago. This is another example of betrayal—a familiar scent associated with the English. During this time period, many Black people were deported to ancestral countries they had never been to or had left as young children. Overnight people were denied access to housing, healthcare, education, employment, or other benefits. This was immensely traumatic and enraging given all that this generation has contributed to the UK. Despite a compensation scheme that has been set up, as of 2023, only 13 percent of the 11,500 eligible claimants have been able to access these funds.[25] This suggests that the compensation itself may be deliberately challenging for people to acquire. My immediate family could well have been impacted by these hostile actions had my grandmother not made a point of acquiring passports for herself and her children because she didn't trust the British government.

This is but a small window into some of the grief we are holding; grief that needs clearing. During these pandemic years, people have been using whatever they can to cope. In the UK a record number of people have died from alcohol abuse due to increased drinking during the pandemic.[26] Based on a survey from *Release,* 50 percent of drug users report that their drug use has increased during the pandemic.[27] This is all evidence of a need to numb, or feel less, when we have few tools we can use to move through the grief.

Barriers to Plant Medicine Due to the War on Drugs

The pandemic has led to a mass awareness of and interest in trauma, mental health, and approaches to "healing." During this, psychedelic-assisted therapies have burst into the public consciousness, the promised panacea on the horizon. I am curious about how psychedelic-assisted therapies can support Black and global majority folks to repattern racial trauma and recover from this. It's one thing to repattern PTSD from war, when veterans are safe back in the country they call home, but what about collaborating with psychedelics to recover from generations of colonial domination and inequality, the legacies of which you must continue to live within?

Western psychedelic therapy protocols, now being developed within clinical contexts and newly regulated in Oregon, often work by support-ing participants to connect with their inner healing intelligence—the part of their bodymind that knows how to heal and come into alignment after trauma, loss, or difficulty has changed their shape.[28] I sense it will be chal-lenging for many Black and global majority communities to trust their inner healing intelligence in a medicalized context after generations of medical apartheid followed by the colonial severing of their traditional approaches to healing.[29] That wound is present and open. A lot more effort is needed to repair, build trust, and practice cultural responsiveness with Black, Indigenous, and global majority communities in the context of psychedelic therapy.

One thing is clear to me: the potential promise of psychedelic medicines will be limited or curtailed for Black and global majority folks if we do not tend to the harms and legacies of the war on drugs. The stigma, fear, and shame associated with the use of drugs or illicit substances of any kind are high due to the trauma of the decades of state-sanctioned violence against our communities. In addition to our communities' lack of trust and the medical community's lack of emphasis on reaching our people, this trauma may be why global majority enrollment into the clinical studies for psychedelic therapy sessions has been so low to date.[30]

In the last decade, I have learnt how the tendrils of the US-initiated war on drugs continues to have a global impact. An example of this is US foreign aid, which is often dependent on countries implementing US-style policies to prohibit drugs. Another example is the way that drug users have been increasingly stigmatized, racialized, and associated with criminality, thanks to the media and the US-backed push for global drug prohibition. In the US, over the last one hundred years specific drugs have been associated by the state with certain racial groups to criminalize them, such as opium with Chinese laborers, cannabis with Latinx folks, and crack cocaine with Black people.[31]

Even before President Nixon formally initiated the war on drugs in 1971, the Western colonial project was entangled with drug prohibition. During their colonization of the Americas, the Spanish conquistadors prohibited plant medicines used by Indigenous peoples. In the mid-nineteenth century, Great Britain wanted to sell opium to the Chinese people. When the Chinese state protested, the British invaded and began what we now call the Opium Wars.[32] Ultimately this invasion was a form of social control to maintain economic dominance over China. During the colonization of West Africa, British invaders banned the Indigenous use of plant medicines in countries including Nigeria under ordinances against witchcraft and juju. Again, this served as a means of social control—when ties were severed between peoples and their plant allies, they could no longer work with medicines for healing or for communing with ancestors or the spirit realms that comprised their cosmology. One of the ways the British colonized people's minds was to sever these connections and replace them with the Bible, whilst at the same time stealing the land. Whether in the past or in the present, drug policies are a form of social control. As Kojo Koram reminds us, "the twentieth century project of global drug prohibition has consistently reinforced racial or ethnic divisions within and between the nations of the world."[33]

Growing up in the UK, I viewed the war on drugs and its associated harms as a US phenomenon until it impacted my family, the consequences of which are still unfolding. It is not my story to tell, so I will share the details of the universal story experienced by so many in recent decades.

Every day in the UK, and in other places including the US and Brazil, Black boys and global majority people are stopped and searched by the police on suspicion of cannabis possession. This happens regardless of whether people smoke weed or not. The suspicion of carrying this plant is predominantly used as a justification to harass, intimidate, criminalize, incarcerate, and at times kill Black people.[34] According to data in *The Colour of Injustice,* a report from *Release* in 2018, Black people in England and Wales were stopped and searched for drugs at almost nine times the rate of white people, while Asian people were stop-searched for drugs at almost three times the rate of whites.[35] Between 2010/11 and 2016/17, arrests from drug searches halved for white people but have stayed the same for Black people. In terms of sentencing, Black and Asian people were convicted of cannabis possession at 11.8 and 2.4 times the rate of whites, respectively, despite lower rates of use, numbers that clearly provide evidence of discrimination. In a 2021 report about drug use during the pandemic, respondents mentioned that they had increased police contact, which suggests that the dynamic of stop and search for Black and global majority people has not reduced.[36] Given that policing of personal drug possession has been deprioritized in many parts of the UK, and that stop and search rates have reduced for white people since 2011, the high rates for Black and global majority people highlight the racist and discriminatory application of drugs policing.[37]

Sometimes children are as young as twelve when the police stalking begins—as if targets have appeared on their backs. Associations of criminality paint over the innocence of their childhood and adolescence, which should be a time and space to explore and be free. Instead, it is common for Black and global majority people to be met with physical violence or harm stemming from interactions with the police because of racialized social control wrapped in the guise of drug policies. The trauma and grief of this can have lasting consequences. There is a strong correlation between experiencing police violence and then developing psychotic experiences in those victimized.[38] Unfortunately, there are deep entanglements between drugs policing and the mental health system. Black people are 50 percent more likely to be sectioned under the mental health act in the UK and have their autonomy taken away, often happening at the hands of the police.[39] While in police custody, or under the mental health act, abuse, poor treatment, and death can occur, with Black people vastly overrepresented among the dead.[40]

Historically, "punitive psychiatry has been used to dominate, delegitimize and lock up 'rebellious' people, including political dissidents."[41] In *The Protest Psychosis,* Jonathan Metzl outlines the way that schizophrenia as a diagnosis has been used to vilify Black militants engaging in antiracist organizing, and since the 1960s has been increasingly associated with Black people.[42] Another example of psychiatry colluding with the state to enforce social control is the invention of the diagnosis "drapetomania" in 1851, which pathologized enslaved Africans when they attempted to escape their captivity. It's important to note that some mental health providers and interventions can be supportive to Black and global majority folks, but usually when they reckon with, and intentionally seek to undo, the harmful legacies within the mental health system.

Growing up in a middle-class, mostly white, or so-called "good neighborhood" doesn't necessarily protect you from the harms of drugs policing or the racist mental health system. Drugs policing snatches lives without mercy, and when you find yourself in the police station, or the court house, or the mental health facility by virtue of your melanin, you can be looked upon as if you deserve to be there, or as if it is simply the way of things.

The war on drugs is a war on people. Beyond police harassment, it also impacts employment, access to education, and the ability to parent. Drugs laws break apart families, mirroring the displacement of families that took place through enslavement and colonial expansion. The loss never stopped. Michelle Alexander notes in *The New Jim Crow* that ending the war on drugs will not necessarily end racism, but it will interrupt the main mechanism that is currently being used to harass, criminalize, incarcerate, and at times kill Black and global majority folks on many lands.[43] To end this, we must move towards the decriminalization and intentional regulation of drugs, but as importantly, we must suck and spit out the manipulative poison that has enabled us to be complicit in this hunting of our kin. We must embrace harm reduction and tend to our fear of drugs, altered states of consciousness, and the wounding that has resulted from carceral systems. We must repair our relationships to plant and fungi beings of all kinds.

As Western psychedelic therapy enters the mainstream, and the regulation of cannabis continues to dismantle drug prohibition, we should advocate for and craft policy that repairs harms done to our communities via the war on drugs. Examples of what this can look like can be seen in the work of the Drug Policy Alliance, which has crafted reparative policy in Chicago—for example, with a tax on cannabis sales that sustains a funding pot for those who have been historically targeted by the war on drugs. *Release,* following suit in the UK, has created a paper highlighting what reparative cannabis policy could look like when it comes to market.[44] This is an opportunity to ensure that people are taken care of and have access to a market they may have expertise in or have been harmed by as a result of prohibition and drugs policing. Either way, there is a way to repair, heal wounds, and build something new that can work for all of us.

Reconnection as Antidote to Colonization

Grief work is necessary, but it is not the end goal in and of itself. As writer and Potawatomi scientist Robin Wall Kimmerer reminds us: grief is part of the broader process of repair; restoration of land and our relationships with the more-than-human world are "a powerful antidote to despair."[45] It enables us to clear space, removing the debris of what was, in order to begin to take different actions, guided by what we love and care for deeply. It may take time to get to a place where reconnection feels possible. We have a lot to move through with the aftershocks of colonization, and this process does not have to be linear. Perhaps it is more akin to a spiral? Perhaps it is a process that weaves in circular undulations, folding in, moving us deeper towards moments of unraveling and discovery through sorrow. Perhaps when composted, it can help us unearth greater capacity to feel alive and celebrate the wonder of each breath, to revel in our collective ability to connect, support life to flourish, and feel intimately woven into the web of relationships that underpin the ecosystems we are part of.

Despite living in a society that has bound notions of "progress" with a fixation on writing and reason, I find my heart pulled towards the bodily, fleshy discipline of practice. Embodying the behaviors and rituals that enable me to live in alignment with my values and visions for this life. I have learnt from my ancestors that actions speak louder than words. I honor the ritual of repetition, trying again when I don't meet my intention, resting and seeking solace with loved ones, before I return to that which roots me. Whether I am tending grief, using the Resilience Toolkit, doing yin yoga or meditation, I notice that my daily practices tend to focus on turning inwards, dimming the distraction of the visual, in service of sensing. I have been aware for some time that the West is obsessed with the visual—what we can see—how bodies look; even progress or change is often measured by what manifests physically in the material realm. I recently learnt that in precolonial Yoruba society, and perhaps for other peoples of the African continent, listening was the primary sense that was honored—not just to sound but to sensation and the murmurings of the metaphysical.[46] This makes sense to my body and has given intergenerational context to an approach to listening, sensing, and feeling that helps me anchor to the present moment and notice if my responses are adaptive to the context I am in.

Politicized somatics can provide a map to explore how we can change our shape and move towards full aliveness, how we can repattern conditioned tendencies that link to colonial legacies, or shift habits that may have been useful for our survival but no longer feel adaptive for the textures of our lives, or the world we wish to live in.[47] Perhaps it was safe to stay small and contained as a survival strategy? Somatics can support us to honor the survival strategies we have developed, while also creating more choice and agency in our own lives as well as within the collective. This might include the choice to take up space, to be in deeper connection with land, to respond rather than react, to feel joy sink into our bodies, or to collaborate effectively in a group. Indigenous wisdom and intact cultures are the point of origin and inspiration for many of the somatic practices that now exist in the contemporary West.[48]

What story are your sensations telling you? What are they whispering? When we get curious about the messages our bodies are conveying and invest in learning how to communicate with them, a whole world emerges. Embodied knowledge is a dialect that has faced erasure under scientific rationalism but can be revived and cultivated at any moment. Being with my body, learning how to listen, sensing, trusting my flesh and the ancestral wisdom it carries, has been pivotal. After recovering from years of dissociation due to childhood sexual abuse, I am learning what home feels like in my body, which in turn allows me to connect more with the human and more-than-human kin around me. I am learning what satisfaction feels like. What enough is. How my body articulates desire and longing. What a no feels like in my body and how to offer that with dignity. A daily, political somatics practice enables me to experience more presence, more agency, and to relate in the ways that feel most adaptive in daily life.

In this lifelong journey towards reconnection, three emerging practices provide pathways for me to access the wisdom of my lineage, rooted in and beyond my body: connection to plant allies, tending to relationships, and ritual dance. I share from the messy truth of my own experiments, learnings, and cycles of composting rather than from a place of "expertise." At times, I feel as though I am fumbling in the dark, trying to slow down enough to hear the whisper of these practices, more ancient than bone, traced in the curves of my skin and the folds of my DNA. A memory is in my body, a song that wants to be sung, remembered and re-created anew for these times. I have often fantasized about the ability to experience ritual in the precolonial context of the Kingdom of Benin, to know what the daily rhythms of life would have felt like for my ancestors in Nigeria before Christianity and British rule were imposed. My heart breaks knowing that this intact, precolonial space no longer exists in the material realm—without the present-day entanglement of the West. I am accepting more and more that we can't go back to what was, but I am curious about what we can grow or re-create with the ancestral treasures that remain, within and outside of the knowledge of our bodies. In my growing practices of reconnecting to plant teachers, ritual dance, and relationship tending, I feel a space in which I can reweave and restore some of the disconnection and fracturing that have taken place within colonization and its aftershocks. What are the practices that can help you to reconnect and align in order to share your gifts with the world?

During the colonial expansion of Western nations, it was not simply violence, subjugation, and extraction that took place—relationships to land and relationships between people and more-than-human kin were broken and subverted to support the needs of the market. As Rupa Marya reminds us,

> Colonialism has fundamentally altered our relationships with the web of life, and we are all living with its consequences. When Europe began its pillage of the Western Hemisphere in 1492, Indigenous cosmologies of reciprocity, relationships of care for water, land, and living beings were uprooted, replaced with a worldview animated by domination, exploitation, and profit.[49]

Scholar and environmental activist Vandana Shiva calls the situation we live with now, as a result of colonization, *eco-apartheid*. "Eco-apartheid is the belief that humans are separate from nature, acting as her conquerors, masters, owners. This separation is one of the major drivers of extinction and biodiversity loss."[50]

How can we develop practices and ways of being that reconnect us to the web of life and each other? Practices that repair and grow livable futures, rather than extract and dominate? We have much to learn from Indigenous peoples and intact cultures who are stewarding 80 percent of the most biodiverse regions of the planet—on 22 percent of the land on Earth.[51] If we are serious about recovering from colonization, we must ensure that Indigenous peoples have access to their lands so their reciprocal stewardship can continue. Another way of saying this is: land back!

I hope to learn how to be in right relationship with the ecosystems I am a part of. It is a slow but steady journey for me. The first entry point was my mother introducing me to medicinal teas and plant allies: chamomile to help with sleep, nettle to support with cleansing, passionflower to soothe anxiety. Through developing relationships with plants, I have found that they have become dear friends, healers, and teachers. I am getting better at identifying where they grow and learning how to support them in turn. As a small monthly offering, I provide some of my menstrual blood to the soil to support the land as she supports me every day. I sense that my friendship with plants is leading me home to the soil and reminding me how to befriend it—with increasing curiosity about what it means to craft healthy soil and how to do this in an urban environment. In composting all this grief over the last years, I am feeling a deepening pull to compost matter—to give something of tangible benefit to the soil cycle.

I continue to cultivate relationships with mycelia and plants that alter consciousness. I am forever indebted to these beings that have touched my life with such clarity. They have supported me to shift towards the complexity of wholeness and—in tandem with politicized somatic practice—create behavior change. I do not think these medicines are *the* answer or for everyone. However, I believe that learning to create robust infrastructures of care that can support people to navigate altered states and integrate them will benefit us as a collective. I feel that we have much to learn from Indigenous stewards of medicine lineages and must continue to determine what reciprocity looks like in action rather than words, within the Western psychedelic space.

I am curious to learn more about plant medicines in the precolonial African context. To this day the Bwiti tradition, practiced by Indigenous peoples in Gabon, has preserved their ceremonial use of Iboga—a shrub with bark that has psychoactive effects that is used within initiation, healing, and other rites. I hope more people in the diaspora will research what plant allies their ancestors commonly worked with before colonization. I feel this is an important part of our history that we must reclaim, whilst being mindful of ensuring that Indigenous communities have the priority for access to the medicine on the lands they steward, so that their cosmologies can continue to thrive without exploitative extraction or assimilation. Blessings of the Forest is modeling what this can look like in the context of Gabon.[52]

The West has a tendency to romanticize Indigenous peoples in ways that are lacking in complexity and are, therefore, dehumanizing. This story of ancestor Malidoma Somé speaking to this, referenced by Susan Raffo, touched my heart.

Westerners or non-Indigenous people get very confused about Indigeneity. They carry this idea that being Indigenous is about living in balance with all life, all of the time ... a state of perfect connection. Of course this isn't true. [Malidoma] said that Indigenous people, like all people, misunderstand each other, intentionally and unintentionally cause harm, have bad days. Things get out of balance. The difference is that being Indigenous means that you know the reason you are here is to attend to relationships. Most of our time . . . is spent attending to imbalance among people, between people and other living beings, between all the ways that one life, human or not, impacts and is impacted by another . . . [It] is about taking relationships and impact seriously and giving the time needed to help balance re-emerge.[53]

I hope that we can do the messy work of tending to relationships, knowing that reengaging that muscle is of benefit, not just for us but for our descendants, as well as the web of life. Examples of this include conflict transformation and ecosystem restoration.

Another elder who speaks to the way that life was organized by her people to serve life is Leanne Betasamosake Simpson:

It sounds idyllic, because compared to now it was idyllic. Our knowledge systems, the education system, the economic system, and the political system of the Michi Saagiig Nishinaabeg were designed to promote more life. Our way of living was designed to generate life— not just human life but life of all living things. . . . Stable governing structures emerged when necessary and dissolved when no longer needed. Leaders were also recognized (not self-appointed) and then disengaged when no longer needed. It was an emergent system reflective of the relationality of the local landscape.[54]

A practice that has become exponentially more important to me is my connection to ritual dance—one of my main portals for ancestral communication. I've learned to listen to and commune through ritual and sensations, through the songs and rivers I carry in my body. I have found dance to be a potent vehicle I can use to connect with ancestral guidance and clear out stagnation. When I am stuck or unsure of where to turn, I trust that intentional dance will support answers to come or grief to flow through me. I know this kind of relationship is not new within the African diaspora—this dynamic underpins many traditions that still thrive to this day.

In the book *Dancing Wisdom,* Yvonne Daniel speaks to the importance of ritual dance for African heritage peoples in the Americas, during and post enslavement, for connecting with ancestors, preserving history and cultural identity, and strengthening norms and language with peoples from other African nations.[55] Ritual dance is a way to "restore" balance after challenges or disruptions to the balance of life. "For Haitian, Cuban, and Bahian worshipers, music and dance performance is the offering, and what they receive in return for their offering is embodied knowledge—the remedy for both ritual and social life."[56] The use of drums was banned or restricted at times by European powers during enslavement, colonization, and the years after because ritual drumming and dance practices connect African heritage people to our cosmology, our ancestors, and our power—which was seen as a threat to the new order that was being established.[57] Given this history, events such as Notting Hill Carnival in London contain a spiritual potency that continues this radical legacy of dance rituals as sites of resistance within the Black community. Claudia Jones, a Trinidadian Marxist feminist, founded Notting Hill Carnival as a response to racist attacks that had been taking place against Afro Caribbean folks in England during the 1950s. She also founded the *West Indian Gazette,* the first commercial Black newspaper in Britain which was known for its pan-African and anti-imperialist approach. May we continue to grow intentional containers for dance rituals, community building, and resistance.

Grief tending is an essential component of organizing that can strengthen movements for social change, building upon the legacies of resistance and refusal undertaken by our ancestors that led us to this moment.[58] I hope that collective grief rituals will strengthen our ability to move together in purposeful ways to create safety, belonging, and dignity for all beings. I hope we can use politicized somatics to practice the behavior change we would like to see and cultivate the capacity to repattern the conditions that create harm and suffering in the collective—Nkem Ndefo calls this process *alchemical resilience.*[59] Tending grief has a way of connecting us to both what we love and what hurts, so I hope we will be inspired to build life-affirming infrastructure so that we have spaces in which to rehearse freedoms, outside and beyond the confines of colonial logics.[60]

Closing Thoughts

In moments of overwhelm and confusion I recall the wisdom of poet Nayyirah Waheed, who reminds us to "put healing on the list. the grocery list. the to do list. the night list."[61] When I feel grief arising, I have to put a grief ritual on my list, to make space and time to compost, repattern, feel deeply, and be held in community. If I know a lot is on my plate, perhaps I write down the source of my grief and place it in my grief jar, knowing I will come back to it during my monthly grief tending ritual.

Can you make time to set aside twenty minutes to let yourself cry? Or hold someone you love as they release their pain, without judgment or trying to fix them? How often have you been held by someone you trust and allowed to fall apart? It is a powerful medicine to give and receive this type of care.

We must reconnect to the songs within; the tendrils of embodied knowledge ever whispering, hoping that we will listen, these ancestral treasures that have lain dusty and dormant for so long, relegated to the attics of our minds. Their value has diminished compared to the logic of the West that we continue to dress ourselves in, convinced that if we just fit ourselves into a different shape, if we become "educated enough" and succeed, we may be seen as fully human.

How do we remember the old ways in the gray space? How do we sustain resistance while having the capacity to build new infrastructure? Perhaps it is a combination of remembering and re-creating: embracing the treasures, practices, and intuitive knowledge we hold in order to move towards communal ways of living that feel in alignment with our ancestors and the web of life. Coming home to the land that we are on and restoring our kinship with the plants, the soil, and the more-than-human kin we share space with.

It's taken many years for me to spend time with these ancestral practices; sometimes only fragments remain. I shed tears for the items looted and forgotten. I send praises for the puzzle pieces I can combine to grow new ceremonies. Adaptation can still be rooted in a lineage and legacy of honoring. As Octavia Butler reminds us, God is change.[62] Let us embody the medicine and futures our hearts long for.

THE VIOLENCE OF THE VOID

Grief has become an emergent topic of conversation in many of my friendships. While I was walking with a friend, who identifies as white, they spoke of their desire to do ancestor healing work and the challenge of this, since they had little connection with their living ancestors, let alone the ones who came before. My friend expressed some envy about my ability to connect with my Yoruba, Guyanese, and Celtic ancestors, to know my lineage and be in relationship with it.

This sparked a rich conversation between us about grief, colonization, loss, and the violence of *the Void*—the sense of internal emptiness that many white people feel; a sense that they have no culture, no richness, no ancestral wisdom to connect with or lean upon.[1] It is this sense of emptiness that I believe is the driving force for cultural appropriation and other intersecting harms rooted in extraction and domination. Here's another way of putting it: "So many Westerners are ready and willing to throw their mongrel history over the side for the spiritual smooth sailing they imagine comes with imbibing an 'intact culture.'"[2]

There is a violence in the Void. The emptiness is a hungry, cannibal-like erasure that has consumed many Indigenous and traditional cultures over the last five hundred years. Do not mistake the Void for nothingness—lying beneath are the tendrils of pain, the stories of Empire and conquerors whose ancestors at one point were the conquered. Other manifestations of the Void can be seen in behaviors of domination, whether this is anthropocentrism, ableism, racism, sexism, transphobia, or homophobia. A feature of this space can be the ongoing sensation of being incomplete, of needing "exotic" rituals or cultural practices to take away the gnawing feeling of not being spiritual, kind, or open-hearted enough. People experiencing the Void often have an urge to consume excessively, hoping that the next peak experience will result in a lasting sense of satisfaction. You choose an endless circuit of tantric retreats, festivals, and plant medicine experiences in the jungle, all dressed in the notion of *doing the work;* you pay lip service to oneness but rarely move beyond the dominance of the individual. You take what you need, believing everything to be yours anyway, to temporarily bypass the feeling of emptiness, the Void churning underneath, untouched and unprocessed, strengthened by the need to extract and consume. You get a quick fix, potentially in another dose of peak experience—ignoring the shadow that cries out for integration.[3]

What would it be like to submerge yourself in this feeling of Void—to really listen to what it needs to heal? To reconnect with stories of your ancestors who practiced ritual and moved with the seasons? This may seem lost to you, but their memories live in your body—they are woven into the fabric of your DNA. Try speaking to them and see what emerges. Know that their whispers may at first appear as sensations in the body. This kind of inquiry asks for more nuance than the written or spoken word—it requires deep listening, space, and time to learn the signals or language of the body. The intuitive "gut feeling" is an example of this.

Working with ancestors is also important on an intellectual level as it puts our lives into context. No being is an island. We are created from deep entanglements, rich histories, and lineages filled with joy and loss, trials, tribulations, and triumphs. Our existence is owed to large amounts of intersecting collaboration—regardless of how sustainable or dysfunctional it was; we are alive because a community of people willed and nurtured us into existence. Even on the scale of the so-called individual, advances in microbial science demonstrate that the idea of a "purely human" body is an illusion. Many of our collaborations with bacteria are essential for daily functioning. For example, "90 percent of the serotonin in our bodies—the neurotransmitter that when abundant makes us feel happy, and when depleted makes us feel depressed—is produced in our guts, and gut microbes play a major role in regulating its production."[4]

As many Indigenous peoples, such as the Anishinaabe, know to be true, we are deeply interconnected with all other beings on this planet.[5] The sense of disconnection, or Void, is a wound that needs to be tended if we are to be in right relationship with the earth and our kin. Once we can acknowledge this, we can begin to ask deeper questions such as what harms did my ancestors experience and how does this impact my life? What harms did they perpetuate on others, knowingly or unknowingly? How do these legacies live on through my body and in relation to other bodies, including the land?

In thinking and feeling into the Void, I have become curious about where it emerges from and how it impacts people within my family. I have found it useful to learn more about the construction of whiteness as an identity and the harms that led white people to develop this sense of internal emptiness, having been so separated from their ancestral roots. Three key events have made themselves known to me: the colonization of European Indigenous peoples by the Roman Empire; the witch burning times; and the actions of plantation owners in the 1700s which birthed the white identity as we know it.

The colonization of Europe and Britannia by the Roman Empire led to the destruction of many Indigenous peoples within these lands. I sense that my Celtic ancestors would have fought against the encroachment of Rome with blood and fire as the Romans proceeded to eradicate any spiritual practices that did not conform to Christianity. This was forced assimilation. *Yes, it happened to your people too.* In some ways, Rome was a template or example for the colonial project led by European nations five hundred years ago, as well as for the universalism that is taking place today under the guise of "*globalization*"—this pressure for peoples around the world to assimilate into the logic of the market and the relational dynamics of Western rationalism that come with capitalism.[6]

In *Come of Age: The Case for Elderhood in a Time of Trouble,* Stephen Jenkinson speaks to the impact of the Roman Empire on the Indigenous peoples of Europe. For these peoples, the forcing of Christianity on their culture was the apocalypse—their ancestral practices were banned and stigmatized and they were forced to assimilate into a universal way of living, without authorized access to their ancestral knowledge.[7] Jenkinson claims, "European peoples in the fading Roman period were awash in dislocation, speaking the tongue of their conquerors, already homeless in their home places, traumatized by culture loss, and the Christian missionaries cannibalized that homelessness, and made it a prime attribute of the soul."[8] The cycle of violence continued, with European peoples becoming the bringers of the same apocalypse to many other people centuries later, including my ancestors in Nigeria and Guyana. Both of these legacies live within me: the stories of those recently colonized, as well as the stories of those who have recently enacted colonization. They had forgotten that a similar brutality had swallowed their ways of living some time ago.

The emptiness left by the fading of the Roman Empire led to what are commonly known as the Dark Ages or Middle Ages (roughly 500 CE to 1500 CE). In *My Grandmother's Hands,* Resmaa Menakem references the trauma that the European ancestors of people who identify as white experienced during this time due to widespread torture and mutilation which were akin to spectator sports.[9] Medieval historian Sean McGlynn notes, "Throughout the whole medieval period there was popular demand for malefactors to receive punishment that was both harsh and purposefully terrifying.... Mutilations sent out a message of warning and deterrence.... With few prisons and no police force, severe punishment was deemed invaluable as a deterrent to crime."[10] Resmaa argues that the epigenetic impact of these centuries of mass violence and brutality came to resemble culture for European peoples:

> Isn't it likely that many of them were traumatized by the time they arrived here? Did over ten centuries of decontextualized medieval European brutality, which was inflicted on white bodies by other white bodies, begin to look like culture? Did this inter-generational trauma and its possible epigenetic effects end with European immigrants' arrival in the "New World"?[11]

During the Middle Ages, the witch burning times also created a huge wound and rupture within communities in Europe and later in the newly formed colonies on Turtle Island.[12] Generally those with a comprehensive knowledge of herbal medicine, midwifery, and healing practices, often within peasant communities, were targeted as witches.[13] The witch burning times lasted for more than two hundred years, and they are estimated to have killed over forty thousand women, though documentation from this period is limited, so the number of deaths may have been higher.[14] During this time, a culture of fear arose. Families, neighbors, and communities turned against each other; people began to accuse others just so they themselves would be saved. In addition to those in power doing away with the commons, the place where a community would gather to farm together, the practice of hunting witches was instrumental in shaping capitalism as a system; it helped the powerful form a political and social set of relationships within the economy that denigrates, yet relies upon, women's unpaid and reproductive labor.[15] As a political strategy, the witch hunt was a horrific and effective way to reduce dissent. It served to limit the power that women healers had, to wipe away Indigenous cosmologies and herbal knowledge systems, and to ensure that power over healing the body could be centralized and authorized by the hands of the newly formed, male-led medical profession.[16]

In *Caliban and the Witch,* Silvia Federici speaks to how essential the witch burning times were for the economic elites. The horrible disruption of the witch hunts allowed them to usher in capitalism and regain control after the Black Death. The plague had severely depleted the number of workers in Europe, which had given them more agency to set their fees and working conditions.[17] The church, alongside economic elites, regained power by taking control of women's reproductive labor by forcing them to bear children, whose numbers increased the workforce.[18] Dissent was suppressed through the witch hunts by disciplining or killing anyone who would not conform to this agenda.[19] In looking at our ancestral past, people of European descent cannot avoid this history of pain, betrayal, violence, and a deep severing from land and plant knowledge systems they had once known. It is a painful yet necessary wound for us to touch into—to notice the ways this history has conditioned our bodies and social relationships in the West.

Despite the horrors white people experienced at the hands of one another during the witch burning times, and despite the fear that permeated for generations as a result, some superficial unity was created in the 1700s with the advent of the white identity. Prior to the "eighteenth-century boom in the African slave trade, between one-half and two-thirds of all early white immigrants to the British colonies in the Western Hemisphere came as unfree laborers, some 300,000 to 400,000 people."[20] At the beginning of this period, these European laborers differentiated themselves based on which countries they had come from, rather than identifying as a unified mass of white people. Many were poor and stolen away from their homes to work in harsh conditions on foreign lands, meaning that they had a lot in common with African enslaved people.

> With its rapidly increasing population, religious and royal wars, Irish ethnic cleansing, and fear of rising crime, Britain excelled among the European imperial powers in shipping its people into bondage in distant lands . . . Vagrant minors, kidnapped persons, convicts, and indentured servants from the British Isles might labor under differing names in law and for longer or shorter terms in the Americas,

but the harshness of their lives dictated that they be, in the words of Daniel Defoe, "more properly called slaves." First in Barbados, then in Jamaica, then in North America, notably in Virginia, Maryland, and Pennsylvania, bound Britons, Scots, and Irish furnished a crucial workforce in the Americas in the seventeenth and eighteenth centuries. In 1618, the City of London and the Virginia Company forged an agreement to transport vagrant children.[21]

The white identity came into existence as a means of destroying coalitions between enslaved African people and indentured laborers of European descent on plantations. There were many revolts, notably Bacon's rebellion in 1676, and these were a concern for the economic elites in Virginia, who were outnumbered by enslaved African people, European indentured laborers, and Indigenous people.[22] As a way to address this, the classic tactic of divide and conquer was applied. The plantation owners gave indentured European laborers more power, and this was attributed to them being white and free, rather than destined for servitude—the label given to enslaved African peoples.[23] This created a sense of superiority amongst the now white indentured laborers; it broke apart coalitions and installed the white laborers as middle-manager oppressors on behalf of the planter elite, who were ultimately exploiting them too.[24]

This instilled superiority and the dynamic of being the middleman oppressor for the elite has been passed down for generations, leading to what we still see in the West today—gray-space societies that center convenience and comfort rather than connection and collaboration, who code legacies of domination into notions of safety and order, dictating which neighborhoods are "good" or "bad" and which bodies are regarded as safe or dangerous. I wonder who and what this serves? I sense that economic elites continue to dance jubilantly to this chess game of divide and rule. Ultimately this is harmful to everyone, white people too, who are conditioned to trade their humanity and empathy for little scraps of power, following the rules, staying safe.

On an embodied level, the Void has created a sense of being numb, of being unable to feel deeply or empathize with others who appear to be different than your kin. From the beginning of the transatlantic slave trade to the present, disembodied knowledge has become the dominant social paradigm in the West.[25] *Disembodied knowledge* can be defined as "intellectual knowledge without concomitant integration of somatic, intuitive understanding and the spiritual wisdom their combination yields."[26] It has been viewed as superior and the general public has been encouraged to embrace it as part of progress. *Cartesian dualism* also refers to this mind-body split that has become dominant in the West; it creates a sense that the mind is the essence of who human beings are, and the body has no wisdom to provide other than being a fleshy vehicle for the mind. As a result, we have been socialized to ignore or numb any sensations or embodied signals that convey moral rights and wrongs; instead we rationalize the deep injustice we see unfolding around us.

Somatic educator Madelanne Rust-D'Eye speaks to this pervasive numbing in her series "The Roots of White Supremacy Are in Our Bodies." She notes,

> We must explore the ways we relate to the sensations and emotions that arise in our bodies in relation to our life experiences. Only then can we actually learn to notice, and *feel,* the *Implicit Associations*—the meanings and associations our bodies make, beneath our conscious awareness—that underlie and result in behaviors and attitudes that marginalize others. We must then learn to *tolerate the discomfort* of not acting on these associations long enough for alternative (ideally, more collaborative) relational outcomes to arise. Another dimension of discomfort that I suggested white Allies must learn to welcome is *tolerating the discomfort of emotion*—and of change, and the unknown—moving through our bodies. Being present to these experiences connects us to our own experience of life in all its textures, and makes us capable of acknowledging and truly caring about the life experiences—in

particular, the suffering—of our fellow humans. I shared my belief that this is a requisite energy source for our wholehearted participation in personal and cultural transformation at this time.[27]

I hope these important threads of history, and how they relate to the people who call themselves white, will become widely discussed in the years to come, especially amongst the younger generations. I hope people will begin to reckon with the wounds, take responsibility for the legacies they are entangled with, and repattern superiority, which is built on a house of cards.

When we acknowledge the historical processes our lives have been shaped by, and when we touch into this on an embodied level, we can cultivate the agency to repattern behavior from old wounds and create new stories and ways of being, rather than unconsciously reproducing the violence of the Void. How do we learn to collaborate in a way that sustains the web of life for the next seven generations? This is one of the big questions I am sitting with. One pathway I can see is to acknowledge and grieve the violence of Empire and the Void space that exists in many as a result of it. Feeling into this wound, and allowing it to compost, can make space for us to remember ways of existing that are in balance with the earth. To weave in cultural practices, rituals, ceremonies, and knowledge systems based on collaboration rather than domination. To become accomplices to the mycelial networks that sustain life ways.

The organization *White Awake* does great work with white folks on Turtle Island and beyond to break cycles of domination and violence.[28] Their flagship course, *Before We Were White,* helps people to understand the specific rituals, land practices, and ways of existing that communities in Europe had before they were colonized and later subsumed into whiteness. Understanding this story can work to contradict the narrative of racial inequality being a deterministic outcome of human nature. It can also dispel one of the features of the Void—feeling as if you are without culture or roots. Once you realize that your cultural treasures have also been stolen from you, perhaps you may feel a sense of kinship and solidarity with those who have more recently undergone colonization? Perhaps this realization can be a healing balm which enables you to commit to taking actions that contribute to racial solidarity, interrupting this cycle of harm for yourself and all beings, rather than feeling like you need to be a saviour of others.

If we are courageous enough to face the wounds of Empire, we can begin to address the Void and come back into connection—with ourselves, our ancestors, and life itself. We can remember, on a body level, that we are held by this land and deeply entangled with it. To support life, we must find a way to be in right relationship with each other. We can begin by composting the barriers that get in the way of us tending to our grief. As Aurora Levins Morales says in *Medicine Stories: Essays for Radicals,*

> What we need is a collective practice in which investigating and shedding privilege is seen as reclaiming connection, mending relationships broken by the system, and is framed as gain, not loss ... Deciding that we are in fact accountable frees us to act. Acknowledging our ancestors' participation in the oppression of others (and this is ultimately true of everyone), and deciding to balance the accounts on their behalf and our own, leads to less shame and more integrity, less self-righteousness and more righteousness, more humility, compassion and a sense of proportion.[29]

TENDING GRIEF IS NECESSARY WITHIN SOCIAL MOVEMENTS

The COVID-19 pandemic catalyzed a collective grief experience on a planetary level. As I write this, we are still entangled with the loss, still finding our feet amongst the waves of new illness and disabilities that people are experiencing. All of this is happening alongside a state-imposed cognitive dissonance and forgetting that seems necessary for us to become productive workers and consumers again. In the snap back to being busy, we are being conditioned to bypass the deaths, the lack of care, and the racial reckoning and exploitation that have been laid bare during this time. These dynamics have been taking place for many decades but are now clear for so many to see. We have a lot to grieve. However, we do not have many tools available to us. Given how much grief there is in this moment and how hard the market logics of late-stage capitalism encourage us to bypass our sorrow, in order to get back to "business as usual," it is subversive to give ourselves space to feel deeply, to grieve and be witnessed in this within community.

During this collage of crisis many social movements have been organizing, responding to emergencies, and trying to sustain life. I am grateful and heartened by this solidarity and collective action. However, I sense that many of these movements of courageous beings are not sustainable. There is no time to feel. Organizing spaces are dominated with the logic of rationality; displaying grief or emotions in general is not seen as strategic.

I recognized this within the English movement spaces I was an active participant in during my younger years. It became clear that if I did not tend to my emotions as they arose, I would not be able to stay involved with integrity. An example of this: I remember often being angry and disappointed about the style of leadership displayed by men in many of the movement spaces I was in—they'd talk over femmes in the space, always want to have the final word, or call our ideas naive if they did not agree with our tactics. These experiences reminded me of having to navigate daily sexism in the world.

The pervasiveness of sexism was leading me to feel like I was in a pressure cooker that was about to explode. My anger about this broader dynamic was becoming centralized and projected onto one person within this activist group—to such an extent that I was finding it hard to engage with them at all. In order to get to the point where I could get across my discomfort with the communication style and dynamics at play, I had to feel into the root cause of the grief; when I did, I knew that beyond the actions of this one person, the heaviness of patriarchy was wearing me down, like a weight upon my back. If I had not taken time to be with my grief about the systemic impacts of patriarchy and its effect on my life, if I had not found ways to release in raves and through tears—my chosen form of relief at that time—I might not have been able to find the space or energy to engage with that person. I would not have been able to show up in integrity and find a way to work together that felt more aligned. Thankfully being with my grief enabled me to have a conversation with them which led to their behavior beginning to shift and communication improved between us collectively. Although this is a small example, and not all challenges can begin to shift after one conversation, I share it to demonstrate that our ongoing hurts can dictate how we show up in the present moment and the choices we feel are available to us.

Do you notice how your unprocessed emotions impact your ability to show up or be in collaboration with others? I invite you to take a moment to pause and reflect on this.

Why is it necessary to incorporate grief into our movements? First and foremost, we have much grief to tend to and, like it or not, we cannot continue to compartmentalize—we must create space to bring our fullness into our movement work and find ways to hold that in agreed-upon ways. Tending to grief within social movements can support flexible thinking, conflict resolution, trust building, and somatic transformation within groups. These are factors that increase resilience and create supportive conditions for sustained movement work. I will also explore some of the current conditions that make many activism spaces unlivable, or hostile to transformation, and how we came to exist in a moment where emotions are seen as something to be suspicious of within the context of social change.

Origins

I identified as an activist for a large part of my life, from the age of twelve until a few years ago when it became clear that this label was no longer supportive for me. This desire for change emerges from a deep well within me that knows that things can be more beautiful, that living immersed in care-based infrastructure is possible. My body longs to experience what I have often felt is our birthright: to be supported to live in conditions that create safety, belonging, and dignity.[1] My interest in social change also emerges from the deep grief that I have felt since childhood—the pain of witnessing the choices so many people in power were making that were causing deep harm. As a child, I remember thinking that politicians were stupid and confused; it wasn't until I got older that I realized that much of the misery they caused was by design. I knew in my bones it did not need to be this way and I felt the fire to do something about it.

In my teens I protested regularly and involved myself in movement work around Palestinian solidarity; queer and trans rights; climate organizing; racial justice work; and more recently, drug policy reform. For five years, I led The Collective Liberation Project, an organization that explored antiracist practice alongside embodied mindfulness techniques. In recent years, I have developed work using dance and somatics to explore how legacies of colonization are connected to our bodies.

In most of the movement spaces in the UK that I have been involved in, the approach has been to prioritize strategy and mental reasoning for specific outcomes or actions. This is understandable as a lot of work is done in the moment in response to urgent situations that need attention. However, I felt we were not making time to sense into the body, to feel the emotions present for people in relation to what we were doing or trying to change. The culture was generally to put on a mask, suppress feelings, and then use substances to numb or disconnect from what was emotionally emerging. I also noticed that people would identify a certain way based on their thinking, the books or newspapers they read, or some other mental reasoning, but the activists I organized with often placed very little attention on what people were representing through their actions or their bodies. I found this frustrating and hypocritical.

This dynamic is illuminated well in the essay "How Can I Be Sexist? I'm an Anarchist!"[2] This essay demonstrates how many men on the left were claiming not to be sexist because of their political views but were not paying attention to their daily behaviors, which often demonstrated male dominance, such as repeatedly interrupting women or female-assigned folks when they were speaking; inappropriately flirting, touching, or sexualizing them; or only supporting male leadership around how to construct certain actions. Despite the anarchist idea of prefigurative politics—creating the world you would like to see in daily interactions—I rarely met folks who were practicing this and attuned to the impact of their daily actions rather than just the construction of their thoughts.

I struggled for many years in movement spaces due to this tension between people's politics and their behavior. The posturing became tiring, as did the performance pressure of needing to be the "perfect activist" who has read all the right things. If you failed to meet this archetype consistently, you were deemed unworthy of having an opinion in the space. Overall, I saw theoretical knowledge prioritized over practice. This emphasis on language and speaking a certain way links to the fact that many of the movement spaces I was in were dominated by white, middle-class, university-educated people who had access to social capital through a certain kind of language. As a result of this ethos, many activism spaces in the West can often be cold, unwelcoming, male-dominated, and presented as the *only way* to be radical or get things done.

In my experience of movement work in the West, many of the conditions are not livable and do not sustain collaboration. It is common to see people burn out, and a lot of emphasis lands on the burnt-out individual rather than the organizing culture, which often does not enable emotions to exist or be held with care. I witnessed a lot of chaotic substance use, especially after protests or intense meetings where people didn't know what to do with their feelings. The alcohol or drugs allowed us a way to numb ourselves as we didn't knowingly have access to practices to emotionally regulate together or to process what had taken place. The general communication style was very pessimistic and rife with critique rather than being supportive of what was going well and how to feel satisfied with the efforts being made.

For these reasons and more, the movement spaces I was in were generally unwelcoming and sometimes actively hostile to new people who may not have had the right language or who may have been from a different background. I often wondered: If people don't feel comfortable or they don't even want to be here, how are we going to encourage others to participate in these movements? I often longed for an ethos that met people where they were or, as adrienne maree brown phrased it, "You're not late to the movement. Whenever you get here, you made it."[3] I became genuinely curious about the following: How can we create movement spaces that hold this sensation, rather than ones that force people to enter from a space of not knowing enough and constantly having to prove their worthiness in order to contribute?

The Black Panther party was known for meeting people where they were in order to shift hearts and minds. The members understood that the average person was getting their information from mainstream TV, radio, and newspapers, and therefore public education was a crucial component of movement building. They tended to this in diverse ways including with consciousness-raising groups, conversation, and their iconic newspaper with Emory Douglas' revolutionary art work—*The Black Panther*.[4] The Black Panthers rooted their actions in caring about people and they realized that in order to get their members on the same page they would need to welcome them where they were. As psychologist and poet Sanah Ahsan reminded me, "meeting people in their not knowing is important to grief work—in places of grief there is so much uncertainty and complexity—cultivating authentic, loving relationship in our movements requires meeting each other where we are."[5]

In 2014, I followed my heart and moved to the San Francisco Bay Area, which felt like a breath of fresh air compared to England. It was there that I was introduced to somatics, restorative justice, as well as the healing justice–centered approach of the emerging Black Lives Matter movement. I witnessed movement work rooted in care, practice, and holistic strategy. It was inspiring and caused me to pivot, to trust in embodied approaches that could hold strategic organizing as well as grief, emotional regulation, restoration, and deep care. During this time, I felt myself expand into my complexity, begin to embody my values as practice, and explore my grief, while experiencing more joyful play than I ever had before.

In 2016 I found myself suddenly back in the UK, despite expecting to be in California much longer. My heart was aching for my friends, the sun, and the way of living I had grown used to in the Bay Area. The seeds of wisdom planted in me during that time on the West Coast continued to grow, and I found myself deeply curious about the organizing cultures I had come across on Turtle Island, and how to support similar dynamics to emerge in the UK. What would it take for practices of embodied care to embed themselves among the people of Britannia—on the land(s) that had raised me? In writing this, I continue sowing seeds towards that exploration.

Context

Many social movements in the UK, and around the world, have been focused on policy change alone, operating at the level of governance. It is necessary to work at this level, and many gains have been made with this approach, be this the five-day work week, the right to unionize, or having protections against discrimination in the workplace. However, by emphasizing this pathway as "activism" or the most effective avenue for change, we may be missing out on other dimensions and necessary approaches to social transformation. Many disability justice activists including Mia Mingus and Leah Lakshmi Piepzna-Samarasinha emphasize care work as radical relational practice and highlight the need for this in order to create a more equitable world and dismantle the barriers that marginalize disabled people. Some revered activists, such as Harriet Tubman, often have their disability glossed over which leads to the false notion that disabled people can't be activists. Additionally, many essential roles within social change work take place outside of front lines, protests, and direct actions; for example, healing, childcare, or providing food for organizers. There are many roles that parents and caregivers can take; some view parenting or eldercare itself as a form of activism.[6] Ableism is very much entangled in our notions of what activists or changemakers do and the roles they can play. I intend to deepen my study of disability justice and continue to imagine new possibilities for roles within social change that are not based on able-bodied fixations. The Social Change Ecosystem Map by Deepa

Iyer gives an example of some of the different roles that are part of generating holistic social change.[7] This approach understands that we may move into different roles or hold multiple roles throughout our lives.

In *Embodied Social Justice,* professor and somatic researcher Rae Johnson argues that it is also necessary to consider the relational interactions and daily, nonverbal behaviors that shape culture and reinforce power dynamics, such as racism, sexism, ableism, and other forms of inequity.[8] Our bodies form gestures, make or remove eye contact, or get close or stay far away to signal many things including dominance, submission, or if a person is seen as safe or dangerous, if they are welcome or excluded.[9] Many of these nonverbal cues are happening unconsciously. In order to repattern or shift the often-unconscious behaviors we have, which entrench power, we must become more aware of the body and the shape it takes in each moment so we can begin to respond, rather than react, and begin to choose new shapes and relational dynamics that are more aligned with our values.

Embodied social justice or political somatics can be seen as the practical approach to culture change that mirrors some theorists within the anarchist and Marxist traditions who proposed creating relational shifts in the present moment, rather than waiting for revolution in the form of a one-time, climactic event.[10] These ideas support creating change by shifting relationships and ways of engaging with each other. For example, anarchist theorist Gustav Landauer argued that "the state is a social relationship; a certain way of people relating to one another. It can be destroyed by creating new social relationships; i.e., by people relating to one another differently."[11]

Similarly, the idea of prefigurative politics argues that one approach to change is to relate, live, and grow culture as if we are already within the world we wish to live in. Prefigurative politics "refers to the strategies and practices employed by political activists to build alternative futures in the present and to effect political change by not reproducing the social structures that activists oppose."[12]

Despite these theoretical approaches within anarchist and Marxist spaces that emphasize the power of living the future values and practices you would like to see, many movement spaces in the UK and beyond seem suspicious of emotions or deep feeling within the context of organizing. Grief is an unwelcome visitor. With all the heavy injustice, study, and strategizing that is being done to address state and social harm, grief is the elephant in the room—it's constantly being shoved down, swallowed, drunk, or numbed away so that activists can continue to function in this logic-dominated dance. As counterintuitive as it feels, embracing grief in agreed-upon containers would bring so many treasures to this work. When we set down what is too heavy to carry, it creates more space to think in a flexible way, to orient from a place of love rooted in what we care about and how we wish to operate in integrity. Tending grief can support us to feel more choice and support us to resolve conflicts, build trust, and engage in somatic transformation as a group—changing ways of being that have become automatic.[13] These are all factors that create supportive conditions for relationships as well as sustained movement work.

I am not alone when it comes to feeling that tending to grief has an important role to play in movement spaces and social change. In *Rebellious Mourning: The Collective Work of Grief,* a powerful anthology of frontline stories, activists and organizers, mostly in the Americas, reference how their grief has been instrumental to their movement work.[14] The text simultaneously offers clarity on why we must hold space for grief within organizing and provides case studies about how grief rituals have already been woven into protests. Speaking to their own entry point into grief tending, the editor of the collection Cindy Milstein notes,

I come to this anthology through my own pain, yet it is inseparable from the pain of the world. . . . This pain laid bare much cruelty, some of it systemic, some of it due to socialization. One of the cruelest affronts, though, was the expectation that pain should be hidden away, buried, privatized—a lie manufactured so as to mask and uphold the social order that produces our many, unnecessary losses. When we instead open ourselves up to the bonds of loss and pain, we lessen what debilitates us; we reassert life and its beauty. We open ourselves up to the bonds of love, expansively understood.[15]

During my time living in the Bay Area, I was deeply moved by the way in which the Black Lives Matter movement incorporated grief rituals and vigils into their protests. The incorporation of vigils provided connection and catharsis for those in need of collective grief space, as well as a strategic approach to honor beloveds killed by police, while at the same time demanding change. Seeing hundreds of people with candles and pictures of the dead was visually beautiful and brought out a feeling of collective reverence. Black Lives Matter protests also provide a much-needed container in which to hold the intergenerational sorrow of having to contend with the ongoing grief of colonization in the form of state violence that has been manifesting in various forms for over five hundred years. When people are together with the pain, the isolation that can feel so heavy with grief dissipates and gives way to connection, a space where solidarity can grow and flourish.

In their essay "Grief Belongs in Social Movements. Can We Embrace It?" Malkia Devich-Cyril notes that their unaddressed grief initially caused them to spiral into work as a coping mechanism. Once they eventually did embrace the need to feel it, they discovered that

> grief is not an enemy to be avoided. In fact, resisting grief led to my suffering, while becoming intimate with grief led me to the lesson that grief and joy are inextricably linked. Though generations of traumatic loss can become conflated with deformed expectations, standards and culture, grief in all its forms has the potential to bring us closer to the truth of the world, to make us more tender and more filled with delight.[16]

Most of the organizers in movement spaces I have witnessed in the UK context have not incorporated grief work into their protests or organizing strategy.[17] As a result, many movement spaces can often be devoid of overt joy, pleasure, or sorrow. By suppressing many feelings, other than rage, these spaces can often become places where people feel the need to perform an idealized version of what an activist "should" be.

In recent years, writers involved in movement building have commented on the seriousness of many movement spaces which, they argue, reduces the effectiveness of these campaigns and the length of time someone is willing to be involved under these conditions. In *Joyful Militancy,* Nick Montgomery and carla bergman name this dynamic *rigid radicalism* and argue that it often involves

> The pleasure of feeling more radical than others and the worry about not being radical enough . . . the vigilant apprehension of errors and complicities in oneself and others . . . the suspicion and resentment felt in the presence of something new; the way curiosity feels naïve and condescension feels right.[18]

These conditions create somewhat of a hostile space which is not welcoming to newcomers or those that may not have the "right" language or have read the "right" books. They can also lead to a sense of one needing to perform rather than being comfortable enough to show up and be authentic in the complexity of one's being. Being expected to work hard and perform in addition to not being given permission to experience emotions and exist in our complexity is draining for the activist, so much so that it can lead to burnout. This sentiment is echoed by Nick Montgomery and carla bergman:

> What depletes us is not just long hours but also the tendencies of shame, anxiety, mistrust, competition, and perfectionism. It is the way in which these tendencies stifle joy: they prevent the capacity for collective creativity, experimentation, and transformation. Often, saying one is burned out is the safest way to disappear, to take a break, to take care of oneself and get away from these dynamics.[19]

adrienne maree brown shares a similar argument in *Pleasure Activism,* where she claims that rather than being something to fear, following what is pleasurable to us can enable more sustained approaches to social change and, if embraced, can enhance our lives, movement work, and community spaces.[20] I very much resonate with the idea of infusing movement work with pleasure and joy, as well as grief. What I sense is that there can be a resistance to *feeling deeply* within movements in general—a resistance to having too much emotionality, as if this will disrupt the strategy we need to engage in successful social transformation. It is important to consider how this dynamic came to exist in order to change it.

How Did We Get Here?

Capitalism, colonialism and heteropatriarchy make us sick. Are our responses healing us? Are our actions generating well being for others? Or are we unintentionally reproducing the kind of relationships that made us sick in the first place?

—ZAINAB AMADAHY, in *Wielding the Force: The Science of Social Justice*

How have we come to exist in a context in which the people aiming to create beautiful futures are often doing so in a way that is removed from pleasure, joy, and grief? Perhaps from feeling in general?

It is useful to name the impact that Cartesian dualism has had on the ways we live today in the West. René Descartes is one of the better-known Enlightenment thinkers whose ideas have been pivotal at shaping modernity as we know it. One of Descartes' most well-known phrases is "I think, therefore I am."[21] This speaks to the hierarchy Descartes emphasized in relation to forms of knowledge production and ways of knowing. He believed that the mind is the essence of who we are as humans and that our bodies have no inherent wisdom or meaning other than being a vehicle for the mind. Rational thinking was seen as superior to bodily sensations and the knowledge that comes from emotions. Alongside this, beings that were associated with rational thinking—white, European men—were seen as the most appropriate to lead, govern, and make decisions, whereas those who were viewed as less rational or civilized were seen as needing to be led towards more productive and "civilized" ways of living. This idea, alongside Descartes' sentiments that humans should have dominion over nature, underpinned the Western colonial project.[22] This logic, not limited to Descartes within the Enlightenment period, facilitated and justified hundreds of years of resource extraction, stolen bodies, theft, and destruction of cultural ways of knowing that did not conform to the hierarchy of knowledge associated with rational thinking.[23]

Within these hierarchies, the tendrils of which can still be felt today, the body is associated with the animal, emotional, and superstitious. This has led to a sense that emotions cannot be trusted, that our bodies cannot be trusted, and that any emotional or embodied signals we receive should be ignored if they are not productive. Industrialization has supported this developing ideology that humans should operate like machines—discounting our sensations or feelings if they do not support our ability to work and be a functional, efficient part of the economy.[24]

In *Beyond the Periphery of the Skin,* scholar Silvia Federici notes that

Capitalism has treated our bodies as work-machines because it is the social system that most systematically has made human labor the essence of the accumulation of wealth and has most needed to maximize its exploitation. It has accomplished this in different ways: with the imposition of more intense and uniform forms of labor as well as multiple disciplinary regimes and institutions, with terror and rituals of degradation.[25]

Various methods have been used to discipline the bodies of workers including getting them to do degrading tasks or demeaning work simply so they could get better at taking orders from others and performing as instructed, even when it was detrimental to their health.[26]

In *Rest Is Resistance: Free Yourself from Grind Culture and Reclaim Your Life,* Tricia Hersey of the Nap Ministry speaks to the way plantations and chattel slavery birthed many of the working practices that are normalized in the contemporary Western world.[27] For example, many enslaved women worked in the fields until the moment they birthed, often also in the fields, then shortly after birthing, on the same day, they were expected to get back to work.[28] This brutal experiment in pushing bodies to act like machines can be seen in the current practice in the US where mothers have no federal right to maternity leave—or where many are expected to work through illness. This logic of not listening to the body, and prioritizing productivity above all else, has led to a context in which many feel guilty about resting and feel a sense of shame or guilt when they are not being "productive."[29]

In the broader social context of the West, emotions such as grief or mental health experiences that reduce our capacity to work and be productive are often pathologized or looked down upon. Prolonged grief disorder as defined by the *DSM* is an example of this.[30] This pathologizing of grief validates what Malidoma Somé shares about the Dagara peoples' view of the West; they sense that in the Western context, emotions are suppressed as a means of social control.[31]

This control of emotions and altered states can be referred to as *mental health oppression*[32]—the ways we suppress our emotions or embodied responses because we are, understandably, afraid of having our autonomy taken away, of being institutionalized for displaying signs of emotionality that can be interpreted as "madness." Some of these embodied expressions can include prolonged laughing, crying, screaming, shaking, or trembling. When we express ourselves in these ways, often to regulate or move through the state we are in, we are at risk of being pathologized and labeled as someone who is mad or ill. In the paradigm of pathology, it is rare for our experiences, hurts, or social or environmental conditions to be taken into account as causes or catalysts for our distress, and need for catharsis. Psychologist and poet Sanah Ahsan notes that for decades Western psychology has emphasized individual diagnosis, placing the emphasis on people and their brain chemistry, while ignoring the systemic challenges or oppression, that is directly implicated in their distress.[33]

This is echoed by Mary Watkins and Helene Shulman in *Towards Psychologies of Liberation,* who note that

> By considering psychological problems as primarily individual, psychology has contributed to obscuring the relationship between personal estrangement and social oppression, presenting the pathology of persons as if it were something removed from history and society, and behavioral disorders as if they played themselves out entirely on the individual plane. Instead, liberation psychology should illuminate the links between an individual's psychological suffering and the social, economic and political contexts in which he or she lives.[34]

We need more spaces to allow our emotions to exist, to be witnessed in community, in order to allow ourselves to move toward full aliveness. If we begin to feel more deeply, we will be less numb to what is going on around us and more able to intervene, explore our choices, say no, or acknowledge what we must resist or change collectively.

Another consideration is the impact of intergenerational trauma and epigenetics. Many people struggling for change have lived experience that underpins their desire to live in a different world, with different relational dynamics. Increasing research is demonstrating that those who have experienced ongoing harms or oppression, such as those with ancestors recently colonized, may experience lasting impacts that could pass to their kin. In *Inflamed,* Rupa Marya and Raj Patel speak to this:

> Epigenetic changes are alterations to our genome that do not affect the DNA sequence but do impact genetic expression. They impact what DNA is expressed and how it is expressed. These changes are how damaging exposures—from environmental chemicals to violence—become written onto, not into, our DNA.[35]

The authors note that ongoing chronic stress can impact "our cells, DNA and our children. By making epigenetic alterations to the genome, stresses such as work burnout, economic precarity, hunger and systemic discrimination can create heritable changes in our DNA."[36]

In organizing spaces, people will likely have generational trauma to tend to in addition to the dynamics of their lived realities. It is important to consider this and begin to prioritize space for grieving, for feeling the emotions present, for holding them and witnessing them so that this burden is not being carried in isolation.

Let's bring this back toward movements for social change. Some of you may be reading this and thinking that if people in movement spaces are all grieving together or being vulnerable about their mental health experiences, how are they going to get anything done? To that I would say this is what capitalist economics has drilled into us—that we can only be productive if we are machine-like, without feeling. I do not believe it is binary. I know from my own experience that when I have had space to feel in community it has led me to a deeper sense of trust, belonging, and connection. It does not have to be an either/or situation in which activists are either numb and productive or in their feelings and unable to achieve anything together. There are endless possibilities in the space between, so I urge you to experiment with the formats and frequency that support intentional moments where deep feeling can be held—this may change along with the conditions of the day. My body longs for a model that allows for feeling space, ritual grief, and sensory experiences to come before strategy so that clarity can emerge through the space that has been created by tending grief.

Weaving Grief into Our Movements

Paying attention acknowledges that we have something to learn from intelligences other than our own. Listening, standing witness, creates an openness to the world in which the boundaries between us can dissolve in a raindrop.

—ROBIN WALL KIMMERER, in *Braiding Sweetgrass*

So, what can tending grief do for our social movements? What would it look like to weave this into ways of working? Before I explore these questions it feels important to name the two people who have been most influential in my thinking about grief work and its importance for our times. Malidoma Somé and Sobonfu Somé were Dagara elders, Indigenous to Burkina Faso; both were instrumental in spreading grief practices through the Western world. I was lucky enough to attend one of Sobonfu's grief rituals in 2014 in California, an immersive, durational grief ritual of over five hours that involved a variety of altars, peer-based community support, and drumming throughout. It was a powerful taste of what grief work in the community can look like.

The Dagara people have a very different approach to grief than the Western world. Rather than being taboo or something to hide from public life, the Dagara see regular grief tending as necessary for the health of the community. Within Dagara customs, the entire community is expected to attend a monthly grief ritual because they believe that unaddressed grief becomes harm that impacts the community. As a result, personal grief work is not seen as an individual issue because what can begin as something with limited impact can ripple through the collective if it is not given the space to be felt and experienced.

Within the Dagara cosmology, the suppression of grief in the West means that we have a huge amount of harm spreading and rippling as a result of what has been left alone to fester. It is akin to a pile of rotting food that smells terrible, impacting the environment around it, rather than a well-maintained compost heap that can be used to nourish the broader ecosystem. There is so much pain in modernity, so much isolation, and many people are finding ways to cope with this by numbing it away with alcohol or other substances because existing with all the feelings is too much.

I am not Dagara but I am influenced by their cosmology and approaches to tending grief. When I look at movements that I have participated in and acknowledge that much of the conflict I have experienced unfolded in these spaces, I am curious if a great deal of this arose from unprocessed grief?

Hyperindividualism would have us believe that we are all islands unto ourselves and the actions of our ancestors have no bearing on our lives. However, research in epigenetics suggests otherwise. We often carry some of the stress and traumatic legacies of our ancestors in our bodies, as well as their wisdom.[37] As a result, we may enact and unconsciously perform the same forms of behavior they did in their lifetime due to a host of factors. Therefore, if you are invested in creating a more care-filled and equitable world, it is worth tending to the dirty laundry of your ancestors for the benefit of yourself and the collective.

In *The Healing Wisdom of Africa,* Malidoma Somé notes that "Elders refer to the righting of wrongs as *keeping the house clean for others.* Thus harmony is won through cleansing and through maintaining vigilance. This allows future generations to inherit purity instead of having to repair the damage that irresponsible grandparents or great grandparents have neglected to fix."[38] In doing this healing work, accountability can be seen to deepen relationships, righting wrongs to strengthen the relationship rather than acting out of shame, guilt, or a culture of punishment.[39]

This ability to understand the nuances of our emotional experiences is very important for conflict transformation. It is essential to have a sense of our own emotional landscape if we are to effectively hold space for others; to allow conflict to bring us closer together rather than tear us apart, and to move beyond what Kai Cheng Thom refers to as the *victim-oppressor binary,* which ultimately wishes to put someone into a static box or role rather than holding them accountable while simultaneously tending to all of the conditions which have led to this harm taking place.[40] It is hard because many of us are experiencing violence and exploitation within late-stage capitalism and desire an outlet. However, without mechanisms in place to tend to our grief, we can end up taking our rage out on each other rather than looking to our common sources of exploitation.

In dipping into our grief, we are also reminded of what we love and care about. Martín Prechtel speaks to this in *The Smell of Rain on Dust,* sharing that grief can often be an expression of praise of what we most care about.[41] How would our movement work shift if we were regularly connected to our why—what we love, what we wish to grow or protect? At times the focus on strategy and getting things done can lead to a repetition of doing things a certain way that may not ultimately be adaptive to the moment. By feeling into what is happening, by connecting to our grief and our love, we can reorient ourselves to the moment and adapt as needed to make emergent choices that serve life and are aligned with our intentions. In *Climate: A New Story,* Charles Eisenstein suggests that it would be much more powerful, enjoyable, and effective to engage with environmental justice work out of love for our Earth and the beings within it, rather than out of the fear that we will all be killed.[42] The orientation prescribes different approaches, actions, and outcomes.

Tending grief can support embodied transformation by increasing somatic awareness, opening, and practice. Ultimately this can lead us to behavior change on an embodied level which is a useful tactic and skill for movement folks to have at their disposal as we are often interested in creating new culture or changing it.[43] According to Staci K. Haines,

> Our deep patterns, survival strategies, beliefs, and reactions live in our somatic structures. By this I mean, live in our tissues, muscles, and organs in patterning that includes, but is not limited to, our well-traveled neuronal pathways. These embodied patterns are supported by our habitual practices and are often reinforced by the structures and systems in which we operate; organizations as well as the broader social structures. The embodied or survival-based habits cannot be changed through conversation or thought alone. The language centers in the brain have very little influence over the survival centers in the nervous system and brain. At the same time, language and thought are important. In the big picture we want to align the head, heart, gut, and actions.[44]

Instead of hindering us, perhaps connecting to political somatics alongside grief work can create the foundation for communities of practice that are in deep alignment, and experimentation towards the world we wish to see.

Engaging in embodied grief rituals can lead a group to develop the skills for *coregulation*—the ability of a person or group to calm the nervous system of another person or group in moments of distress.[45] In a context in which people are open to grief and can detect embodied signs of distress, consensual interventions can be offered, such as inviting a person to release sounds that represent their feelings, shake if need be, or receive supportive touch. Skills from grief tending can be applied to other moments when care is needed, deepening trust within organizing contexts.

Tending grief is also a mechanism for building trust. If someone can hold space for you at your most vulnerable, you are more likely to feel deeper solidarity and camaraderie with them in situations when the stakes are high. Grief rituals also enable moments of slowing down so we can be present without bypassing, and choose collectively to acknowledge what is present even if it may be challenging.

Grief also connects us to something we all universally share—the process of loss. As Audre Lorde reminds us, it is important to celebrate our differences, yet simultaneously I feel it is powerful to acknowledge what is true for all of us.[46] We will all die. We will all have to be separated from those we love and may struggle when these things shift. We have much to gain by learning to hold space for these transitions which are near universal for all of us.

Tending grief can support flexible thinking, conflict resolution, trust building, and somatic transformation within groups, which are all factors that increase resilience and create supportive conditions for sustained movement work. I hope that the grief rituals in the latter part of this book can weave their way into movement spaces so we can reclaim our ability to feel, be in connection, and move towards aliveness, as we grow the worlds our hearts long for. Some practical ideas to experiment with could be hosting a monthly grief ritual in your community, or doing this on a smaller scale in a pod of chosen people, or even beginning to experiment with creating some space for twenty minutes for a grief check-in to see where people are and what is on their hearts before going into a meeting.

I hope that social movements will warmly embrace grief work as a generative thread within organizing. May we move with integrity, rooted in love rather than scarcity, making strategic and skillful use of our anger, so we avoid domination. May we grow holistic movements that can sustain us, be experimental, and embrace all our parts.

A CONVERSATION WITH AISHA FROM *MISERY* ABOUT GRIEF WORK WITHIN THE CLUB CONTEXT

Aisha Mirza is a multidisciplinary artist, writer, DJ, crisis counselor, and community worker living between a boat in East London and an apartment in Brooklyn, New York. They are Pakistani and Egyptian, and were raised on an estate in North London. They have worked in the emergency room of New York's biggest and oldest public hospital as a sexual assault and domestic violence crisis counselor. They have also worked as a social worker for a radical mental health housing provider in NYC.

In 2019 Aisha created *misery,* which is a mental health charity and sober club night based in London that is devoted to healing for queer and transgender people of the global majority. Mental health is at the center of their work as they have a bunch of experience being really fucking sad. They remain devoted to the otherworldliness of madness and to imagining a society that could hold, honor, and learn from it—a place where it could grow, become something else completely if it wanted to.

Camille:

How did the idea for *misery* emerge?[1]

Aisha:

misery started in 2018 as an idea and it eventually formed into our first event in 2019. It started for several different reasons. I have always worked in mental health in some kind of capacity, but I was slightly tired of working in trauma response, which is where I had been for the years prior. I was a bit burned out from that, but I still knew that I wanted to work on some kind of mental health project because that is where my heart is.

I was trying to think about how I could start something that would feel nourishing for me as well. As someone who loves nightlife, music, and the club, the idea of blending nightlife and mental health intervention felt aligned. Another part of it was having lots of friends and knowing people in the wider community with substance-use issues. I was starting to feel quite saturated, as a friend, in terms of how much I could personally hold while being out enjoying a party.

Most of the queer parties were the same sort of space, centering a specific kind of hedonism related to fashion or being an extrovert. I got a little bit wary of the scene and the cycle of getting really fucked up in those spaces and then feeling suicidal on the Monday afterward. This was the cycle that I was seeing among a lot of peers and some close friends as well. Through conversations, we started thinking about what it would be like to create an alternative nightlife space. Clearly, queer people need and love the club, but we wanted to provide an option that centered care and supportive mental health practices.

I had an acquaintance-type friend that I was talking to on Facebook Messenger around that time, and they were suffering with their mental health. We were trying to plan a meetup and they were saying, "I wish there was somewhere I could go and be with other people, but I don't feel like I can because I'm just so depressed. I wish there was somewhere I could go as I am," and I was like, "Oh, my God, we should start something, like a depression club, a place where you can go and just be depressed together." This connects to one of our original tag lines which is: "You can cry if you want to."

Very fucking tragically, this friend ended up taking their life a couple of weeks after that conversation, which was a big motivator for me in terms of really making sure that *misery* happened. They are infused in the fibers of the whole project because they named something important, which was the need to have a space to go where you can take all your parts.

I suppose that is where the idea for the club night was born, which is where we started as a collective. It became clear that to create an actual mental health intervention for our community at this time, it would need to be sober. Not because we are trying to force sobriety on anyone—we try to be careful to avoid shame-based language around substance use. It was more about the realization that sober spaces are just not available for our community. Having options is great, so we decided to provide a space, where people could have a fun, queer, cunty nightlife experience, but be sober for it.

Camille:

Thanks for sharing that. Was it challenging to find a venue that would let you rent space without running an alcohol-based bar?

Aisha:

Yeah, it took us about six months to find a venue that was willing to work with us for this first party because it is a loss for a venue in London to throw a sober party. We were being offered Tuesday nights or Wednesday nights, but we felt very keen for this to be seen as a legitimate option within the community on a Friday or a Saturday night, rather than as an aside. Mental healthcare can sometimes be seen as an afterthought despite it being central to what everyone needs. We stood our ground, and then finally were offered a Friday night spot by a venue in East London. The leadership of the venue definitely had some gays in it, which swung it in our favor. I think they saw the point of what we were trying to do.

You opened that party, that first-ever event with a somatic, trauma-informed movement workshop, with a great bass soundtrack.

Yeah, it was such a vulnerable moment. Thinking back, we were like, "Let's try this thing out. Let us step into this space where we do not know how it is going to go or how it is going to be perceived. Are people coming or not? Is it needed or not?" Honestly, it was one of the sweetest moments of my life, opening the doors to that party and just seeing this string of depressed young people walk in and stand in a slightly awkward circle around you, while you guided them through this movement workshop. It was so sweet.

It is good to reflect on that moment and notice that the *misery* community we have fostered over the last four or five years has the same heart and essence that was present in that initial workshop. It is very gentle, unassuming, brave, vulnerable, and different from what I had come to know as, or what the corporate brands push as, the idea of queer community and the type of energy that comes with that. It was incredibly soft.

Camille:

Yeah, it was such a joy to participate in that space. It was exactly what I was craving, as I was in a deep-grief moment myself and in need of softness.

How has *misery* developed over the years, particularly during the pandemic when club events could not take place?

Aisha:

We have grown more strands to the work. Our other main offering developed during the pandemic, during lockdown, with some of the lessons from that time. When it was sanctioned to meet outside again, we created spaces for queer and trans people of color to be together in nature and learn how to identify and forage medicinal plants to support wellbeing. We would meet in green spaces in London alongside herbal medicine practitioners who could show us how to make some connection with the plants and the nonhuman life around us. Obviously, nature-based mental health work has been done for centuries as it is so good for our spirits.

I found the pandemic and the lockdowns to be an almost spiritual time. There were a lot of lessons that happened during that time that I did not want to lose in this great getting-back-to-normal wave that we are in now. That inspired some of the work that we are currently doing. We still have the party element, which is really successful and lovely. Our most recent party sold out at around three hundred tickets, which, again, for a sober party that is centering our community of queer, trans, Black, and people of color is amazing. The need for it has been proven and the support has been extremely vocal and present from the beginning in a beautiful way.

Camille:

I feel that club culture can be transformative, but with the commodification of it, it is increasingly about seeming cool or dressing a certain way rather than getting free. I am wondering what your thoughts are around the club as a container for repatterning trauma or working through challenging emotions?

Aisha:

Yeah, nightlife in general is a funny one—I love it, but I recognize that it takes so much for me to feel comfortable and able to participate. A lot of the time, the way that nightlife has been set up is that you must in some way repackage or push down certain parts of yourself to be in the space. Especially, for people who suffer with more intense mental health challenges and different ways of being. Nightlife centers a certain kind of extrovertedness, the celebration of feeling comfortable taking up space, and all those things are amazing, but there is still a need to provide some quieter spaces. We also need spaces where madness is allowed, and I suppose that is what we were trying to do. There is no easy or specific way to create that space, but we are trying.

One of the moments we started to realize the need and the impact of having that kind of space available was when someone had come to a *misery* party from outside of London and they mentioned to one of the facilitators that it was the first time they had felt comfortable wearing short sleeves because they had self-harm scars on their arms. I felt happy to hear that story. That is exactly the type of space we are trying to cultivate, where that part of yourself that you might have felt inclined to cover up before going out is welcome in the space and celebrated as part of who you are.

Camille:

What mental health interventions or supports do you have at a *misery* party?

Aisha:

We realized if we were going to take substances out of the equation, we needed to compensate for that in some ways, as a lot of people rely on drugs to feel comfortable, or more extroverted, so they can participate in the space or go as long as they want to. We offer a diversity of experiences to try and suit different types of moods. These can include coloring exercises, nail painting, movement workshops, and a zine library to name a few.

We are trying different options, which seems to have worked well. Most of our community cannot afford mental healthcare in the way that people deserve to have it and there are so many other barriers. Our aim is to create a space that has the party element and offers a lot of what the party offers but also introduces our community to therapeutic ideas and basic supports like sitting and coloring which can be so basic, but if you do it in the right moment, it can really change things for you as it's so soothing.

A few months in, we introduced the talking space element of it. Now, at all our bigger events, we have a therapist, mental health practitioner, or a community worker who feels comfortable taking the role of holding space one on one at the party. It is a flexible space and role. It can be a listening space or, if necessary, more of a signposting space, a space to talk about how that person might access more support or help. I really love that addition, too. We are experimenting with all of that to create, and to widen the scope of, what a party or nightlife can be for people.

Camille:

It is so powerful to hear you speak about introducing people to different mental health supports in a peer-based, communal model. Therapy can be great, depending on who you are working with and if you find the right fit for you, but it is not accessible to many people. It is only within the last three years that I have had enough money to see a therapist on a regular basis. In my teenage years, when my depression was intense, I used clubs and raves as therapeutic support or emotional maintenance. It gave me space to shake out some of the feelings and get the energy to face another week. Many people use the club in this way, consciously or unconsciously. To be introduced to more resources to support mental wellbeing in that context is so clever and so needed. I love it, conceptually.

Aisha:

Yes. That is a good way to put it. It has always been a therapeutic space, right? It is just about teasing that out a little bit as well.

Camille:

What do you think the connection is between grief and mental health?

Aisha:

That is a big one. I used to have a limited idea about what grief was or who could feel it and it was very much connected to death. What I have realized through my work in mental health, with *misery,* as well as through your teachings, is just how much grief is infused in every-day life. That does not have to be a bad or scary thing because to have love is to have grief as well. Both emotions are part of the fabric of everything.

It is a weird colonial rewriting for us to feel that grief is this thing that you only experience when someone dies and then you get over it. I am currently in this very charmed position of not having yet dealt with the death of someone very close to me, so I always felt like I had escaped grief. When I started exploring that more, my question was "How could I be so sad all the time?" I have not even experienced one of life's greatest challenges and forms of loss. Though once I started to understand that everything is infused with grief, particularly for those who are marginalized or oppressed, there is grief inherent in what has been taken from you, from the unjustness of life.

Also, a way of understanding why I felt so much grief without having experienced much death was thinking about it specifically in the mental health context of grieving versions of yourself, or the grief you might feel for the nineteen-year-old version of yourself who was in so much pain and had absolutely no idea what to do. That was such a scary place to be. I accept that fifteen years later, I might still carry the grief of that earlier version of myself, as well as ancestral grief or inter-generational grief. Allowing yourself to believe that some of what you feel and carry might not be directly yours, but is an accumulation of the grief and horror experienced one, two, or three generations ago, can be liberating.

That was my journey with grief and mental health. Relearning what it means, why I might experience it, and why our community might always live in a bubble of grief, actually. In thinking more about it I see how little space there is within our capitalist societies to honor grief. I wonder where it goes?

It is funny that these revelations feel quite recent for me, but it is amazing to figure out the language for some of those huge feelings. I am fascinated by how grief is approached, supported, and managed in various places in the world. To use the language of the colonizer, it feels backward to have no space for grief in the way that we do in our high-flying "first-world society." It is so essential.

Camille:

Yes! I would really love to have a regular, communal space for grief because it is an ongoing thread that needs tending.

I do not find mental health pathology useful in many contexts, but in the last year, I have been reclaiming my relationship with depression after years of not really acknowledging it. I notice that when I start to feel depressed or flooded with sadness, it is an indicator that I need to make space for a grief ritual. I am not claiming that depression is universally unprocessed grief, but for myself, I notice a deep connection between the two.

Aisha:

At our last party in August, the summer fair, we did have a grief space, which was the first time we had ever done that or named that specifically. That was a bit scary because we put "grief space" on the flier and then, the party is approaching and I am like, "What the fuck? I don't know what to do for a grief space." I was freaking out because people really responded to it. They were like, "Oh, the grief space? I'm excited about the grief space." I was like, "Oh, shit, I can't pretend that we didn't put that in now." People are into it. People need it. In the end, I, and my partner, Soha, ended up knocking something together. We actually put a lot of thought into it. We facilitated a write-your-grief exercise because we were thinking about how to transform everyone's individual grief into a visible, collective collage, so we ended up doing the three stages of the butterfly: the caterpillar, the cocoon, and the butterfly. We pasted these big cutouts onto the wall, then with lots of colorful paper, we asked everyone to write out some of their grief and stick it on one of the stages of the butterfly lifecycle. Part of the exercise involves noticing and choosing which stage you feel your grief most belongs to, then coloring the paper in, so by the end, they all looked different. Everyone's grief gathered and decorated with care. It was beautiful.

We set this up in a corner somewhere outside. We had candles and incense, and there were a lot of people as the night went on, sitting by it, crying. I felt good about people having this space. I would like to develop the idea a little bit, but it was amazing to see how the community responded to a small offering, built upon it, and made it what it was supposed to be.

Another thing to remember when holding or engaging with grief spaces is that it can feel so big, so it is important to be easy with yourself and know that even the acknowledgment of it or opening the door and looking at it before closing the door again is all good work. The grief retreat that you facilitated, which was life-changing work, provided a model for what that space can look and feel like. There were so many little bite-size, manageable chunks offered to get at this thing that can sometimes feel so intense and all-consuming. I really appreciated that because it became less daunting and easier to engage with.

Camille:

Moving toward making it part of daily life.

Aisha:

Yes, exactly.

Camille:

That is my goal. I am not there yet, but I am taking small steps.

Aisha:

I think even naming it is huge.

Camille:

Yes. Also having permission to acknowledge that grief exists on this systemic level as well. I know we have good chats in our circles about moving beyond individualism, but when it comes to our own experiences of hurt, grief, or mental health, there is still so much individualizing of it, rather than noticing and highlighting the collective impact for so many of us. There is a power in having our grief named in public space, connecting the dots, and saying, "This isn't just you. There is nothing wrong with your brain chemistry. This is something that we are all navigating because our society is not structured in a way that supports us to be well."

Aisha:

Yes! We have a few little catch phrases that we will throw in at *misery* such as "You're not crazy. It is mad out there." Holding that mirror up. I was lucky to study with a lot of radical mental health people in New York quite early into my training and that is the central idea there around mental health work, that it is not actually a sign of sickness to feel unwell in this world. If you take a second and look around, it is an appropriate response to the situation.

People are starting to get that. It is becoming much more accepted, and people are more allowed to claim that for themselves. There is this individualization bit and an aspect with people not allowing themselves to claim things outside of themselves as something that they suffer with, too. A sense that those structural issues cannot be affecting me that much. It must be something within myself.

Camille:

I have been thinking about our more recent ancestors, parents and grandparents who went through colonization, migration, or displacement. Many of these experiences within my own family are entangled with grief, whether people are available to look at it or not.

What are your thoughts about how colonization, oppression, and migration link to grief?

Aisha:

God, just in every way imaginable. There is so much there. As you were saying, too, I think I have just started to allow myself to think about ancestral grief and events unknown to me as being part of my experience of the world and mental health. I think it can get to a point where we are encouraged with our own specific mental health to break ourselves down into so many little pieces to try to explain or justify certain behaviors.

It became clear to me in my own journey that those answers were not there. You can look as hard as you want, berate yourself, and do as much psychoanalysis as you want, but there is an element to mental health that is whimsical. It is energetic. It is spiritual. It is stored in places that we do not necessarily have access to, so that has definitely brought me a lot of peace in my journey, knowing I may not find all the answers.

It is okay to honor the feelings that you have, be it grief or something else, without knowing why it is there, and just accepting that, yes, being queer, trans, a person of color, children of immigrants, child of poverty, that is plenty. All those things are infused with huge grief. I mean, you can start locally in that way, but I have a habit, I guess, of zooming out far to also consider things like the grief wrapped up in greed, or all the harms that led to the world we live in now. There is so much there.

Camille:

Do you notice a generational divide when it comes to exploring mental health?

Aisha:

I feel like I honestly have not had enough interaction with older generations to be able to speak on it. I am inclined to say it really depends.

In thinking about *misery,* we have queer elders who come through who totally get it. I think queer and trans elders have a different viewpoint on this stuff. Generally speaking, there does tend to be much less space for mental-health-type stuff in older generations. Be that through cultural differences or not. There is a lot of a get-on-with-it–type attitude that can be found in older generations, which is always surprising to me because I am like, "How did you guys do that?" Obviously, the mental health shit was still there, right? It is not like you all just did not have it. Where did that go? We know. We know where it went.

I would love to see and hear more examples of people from older generations who did have a different approach or refused to just get on with it.

Camille:

I am also interested in learning more. I have a sense, based on the people in my family context, but, yes, I agree that it is best not to make sweeping generalizations. The LGBTQ+ ancestors who survived the AIDS pandemic experienced so much loss and oppression. It makes sense that, as a result, queer elders would be more tapped into grief work and mental health interventions.

The internet is such a huge factor as well. I share this noticing about elders with a huge serving of compassion because if you do not have access to information to do something differently, what are you going to do?

Aisha:

Definitely. The intergenerational stuff is super underexamined. I think we would all benefit so much from that, but then, on the other side of things, I was talking to a friend yesterday who's a therapist at an elementary school, and they were saying that they were talking to this girl in fifth grade, who's like ten or eleven, and she basically named all of the stages of grief and told him which stage she was currently experiencing during their conversation.

Camille:

Wow. What are your most glorious visions for a world where people's need for communion around grief and mental health are met?

Aisha:

This is something I struggle with. It is hard to imagine a future where the things that we are working on or striving for are abundant and met without seeing a total reframe of literally every system that currently exists. A world where mental health needs are met would be a world where people do not have to prove themselves through productivity to have access to basic things. Everyone would be housed. Everyone would be housed alone if they wanted that.

Things would be done on some kind of global volunteer system to keep things running to nurture the land and everything that we would need, but everyone would have their needs met without question. That is really where we would have to start, I think. In that glorious future vision, the work we do would not be necessary in the way that it is now, it would be play. It would be much more spacious, creative work. Not creative in the face of scarcity and oppression, but creative in the sense of looking at all these people and creatures with all these things to offer and ways of existing in the world and this dream space that they are able to tap into every day because all their energy is not used for survival.

That is the work that we would be doing. It would be frolicking in that dream space and making things even more beautiful than they already are. Our energy would go toward supporting and learning from folks with mental health differences, going back to a space where people of different mental experience are like oracles and know something that the rest of us do not know, and they are treated as such, upheld in that way, and cared for.

I do not see a glorious future within capitalism because I personally do not believe that mental ill health is something to be managed or molded into day-to-day, productive living in the way that society at large might be doing it. I believe that people who are considered to be mad or mentally ill have gifts. We are tapped into something special. That is what I believe, so a world where that was respected would be ideal.

Camille:

Yes. Power to that.

Aisha:

Part of the gift is not being able to turn your back on the grief that runs like a river through life and through the world, through the energy of every day. I know, for me, taking antidepressants or whatever else it has been over the last decade, narrows my focus and reduces my ability to tap into huge feelings. Wells and wells and floods of feeling. My choice to take those medications is a choice to reduce my senses because it is just not convenient for me to be tapped into all of that while navigating capitalism. So yes, a world where you did not have to fear that, but you were supported in holding the feelings.

Camille:

Thank you so much. I trust we will do what we can to move in that direction. Step by step.

A CONVERSATION WITH ZACHI FROM DOPO ABOUT ABORTION COMPANIONSHIP AS COMMUNITY GRIEF WORK

Zachi is a Black, queer human and founder of Dopo, an abortion support and education community and cooperative.[1] As an abortion companion and reproductive justice educator, she supports individuals through transitional experiences, builds communities around our shared stories, and advocates for a messy revolution based on care, justice, and our collective dreams. In true millennial style, she is a multihyphenated professional, juggling a range of roles across various organizations, with a focus on reproductive justice, LGBTQ+ wellbeing, and mental health. She is a Londoner but lives part-time with her partner in Italy.

Camille:

In 2017, I had an abortion for the first time. In the weeks prior, I was looking for a Black or global majority abortion doula in London, with awareness of how to support nonbinary people in this context. I could not find anyone who matched my needs. When I heard about Dopo, some years later, I was so happy because you are providing exactly what I was looking for and I appreciate how many people will benefit.

Could you share what an abortion doula is and what kind of support you offer?

Zachi:

Thank you for affirming and introducing this conversation. Abortion doulas or abortion companions, as I call myself now, do many different things. We accompany someone along their abortion experience— whether that is before, during, or after—with various interconnected pillars of support: emotional, physical, or spiritual. This all enables planning and care around the abortion experience.

Emotional support is the umbrella under which all the other forms of support fall. If you are helping someone plan the organization of their abortion, they may need to take days off work, plan to have food or meals in the fridge, or know where to call to make an appointment. Although practical, these are all forms of emotional support. We also help people to consider how to stay in touch with their body during the process or manage pain, as well as with any mental health and spiritual considerations they may have. In short, an abortion companion is someone who provides various forms of emotional support for people who are planning to or considering having, currently having, or have had an abortion (recently or decades ago).

I believe that anyone can be an abortion companion. The reason I use companion and not doula, is because the word *doula* sometimes has a certain status attached to it or has connotations around who can be in that role and who can access support, leading to even less accessible care, especially for those experiencing multiple intersecting facets of marginalization. At the core, companionship is what most of us who have had, or are in the process of having, an abortion are seeking. I do not think you need training to be a companion. You need confidence, and training can help you with confidence.

Camille:

Can you say more about your training at Dopo and how folks can hold space for someone having an abortion if they choose not to attend a training?

Zachi:

When I started in 2016 or 2017, I did not do abortion doula training. The closest I could find was birth doula training, so I decided to transfer the skills and root my approach in my own experience, creating what I needed at the time.

I think one of the most valuable skills for a (trained or untrained) companion is self-reflection. Building a practice of self-reflection as a companion, or support person, will put you in the best position because it allows you to remember that it is not about you and your role; it is more about centering and being guided by the people that you support. When the dynamic of the relationship is like that, that is when you can be most caring. That is when you can be most genuine. That is when you can be the most human rather than moving from superiority, thinking that as a doula or companion, you know better.

In the Dopo training, we share a lot of anecdotal learnings from our own experiences as abortion companions, and we have modules on what abortion is, helping people to understand the process, especially if they have never been through it themselves. What does practical support look like if you are with someone virtually or in person? How do you help someone plan logistically for abortion? In the end, all our contexts are different, so we teach from as wide a perspective as possible, understanding that every community and individual has unique needs.

The crucial moment where I see a big change in people is when we do a values exploration exercise, asking people to anonymously respond to questions and see how they sit with them. This prompts participants to consider how they show up for people. That is the most transformative part of the training.

Camille:

Since having my abortion, I have felt a lot of guilt about how I supported a close friend at university through her experience. At the time, I had a limited understanding about what people can emotionally or physically go through during abortion; I was given little information about it growing up. Looking back, I feel that my care could have been more nuanced.

If someone has received limited information about abortion, what are some of the best practices to be a loving support to someone going through it?

Zachi:

The first one that comes to mind: Avoid rushing. I think the way we talk about abortion in the UK is that it is very much about choice. Over the last few years, I have learned that people make decisions, but they are rarely this clean choice that abortion is framed as in this pro-choice ethos. When it is framed as a choice, many people that have never had an abortion are like, "Well, you chose it, so why aren't you happy?" This line of thinking is also limiting for people having an abortion who can end up thinking, I have made this decision, so why is my world falling apart?

Another thing: Do not have an end goal of how you think that person should feel or the steps they should take to feel anything at all. Be extremely present when they share their grief. Witness when they are like, "I'm so relieved and I'm actually so happy. Let's go out for a drink or let's go for a bike ride or something." Know that when you are speaking to them the next day, a week or a month later, their feelings could be completely different. You being present allows them to explore whatever that emotional journey is for them without feeling any pressure that they have to be better, not in pain, or not confused. It is about holding an open space for anything that is true for them at that moment. This can make a real difference.

The last thing I will say about this is be mindful of time. Check in with people, even if it has been six months, even if it has been a year or two years. Ask, "Hey, how are you feeling about that?" For most people, at least everyone I have spoken to, the experience does not leave you. It can be extremely comforting to have someone check in about the emotional side, which is the thing that lasts the longest.

Camille:

Thank you for that. My nineteen-year-old self is so grateful and would have loved to have this information at the time. Hopefully, people who read this can have something to hold lightly as a way to approach support.

Could you share more about how Dopo emerged?

Zachi:

I worked alone for a few years and, as I mentioned, I hadn't had any abortion doula training. I was doing okay, but I was also feeling quite stretched doing the work alone without other people that aligned with me in the UK. In the US, I knew there was a huge abortion movement, but it seemed very rights based with many of the abortion doulas I knew working mainly on logistics in the clinic or for abortion funds. I didn't see many people focusing mostly on the emotional side of things.

After a few years I realized that I needed community. I had my abortion alone and becoming a companion was a way to prevent other people from being alone in the experience if they did not want to be. Yet I found myself alone as a companion. So that is how Dopo started, from a desire to not do this alone and believing that abortion should be a communal process, if desired. We all have the power to improve care for each other, for ourselves, and for that, we need community. So that is why Dopo emerged.

The name *Dopo* means "after" in Italian. I chose it because there is so much focus on getting to the point of having an abortion and then a vacuum of space after; or that is how I felt. Our focus, in name and approach, is about improving the situation after, whether that is through education, care, or training people. The aim is a better situation after abortion.

It has been a year and we are a registered cooperative. We chose that model so the format can reflect the communal ethos and allow us all to dream it into being. To imagine: What can abortion look like in community?

Although I started it, I do not think it will continue with me leading it in the long term. I do not want it to end with my vision. We all have the capacity to decide as a group and to work collectively to build a new future for what abortion support looks like.

Camille:

What a beautiful stewardship model. It sounds to me that instead of tightly gripping, you are creating the container to allow Dopo to flourish and grow in the ways it needs to, which is powerful leadership. Thank you for doing that. May more people follow your example in the years to come.

Zachi:

Thank you. I like the word that you said, stewardship. A personal struggle I have is that it is so difficult to know how to allow things to flourish naturally. I do not want to be the one thinking, okay, how to do this? I want it to be organic, but it is a process, and I am doing my best to trust it.

Camille:

According to 2019 statistics from the Department of Health and Social Care, over 49 percent of women or people assigned female at birth (AFAB), over age thirty have had at least one abortion in their lifetime.[2] Despite how common this experience is in the UK, it is still so taboo to discuss in public, let alone acknowledge the impact it can have in our lives. I felt a lot of rage and grief about how hidden it is from public life and the unspoken pressure to hide in a corner and deal with it alone.

Given this context, I see Dopo as community grief work. Does that resonate with you?

Zachi:

Yes, I agree because grief is the most common emotion people share with me. For people that have not had abortions or do not have these conversations, they can assume, "Oh, you're grieving because you made the wrong decision or you are grieving the baby," which can also be true. What they miss is the grief of having to do it alone; the lack of space to have these conversations. The grief of wanting to parent, but not right now, and being upset that it happened in this moment. There is the grief of our bodies: I was not meant to be pregnant at all, why was I pregnant? Or feeling that our bodies have failed us. The grief of unsupportive partners, and those who may not want the pregnancy to go on. The grief of not being in partnership, the grief of being in a partnership that feels all wrong, and the abortion brings all of that up. All those statements can be true in different contexts for each of us. There is so much grief and it is often unspoken.

Part of what we do at Dopo is have all these conversations. We hold space for people who have terminations after twenty-four weeks because of a medical diagnosis as well as people who just do not want to be pregnant anymore but do not want to be alone. There are so many stories, and we can all have these conversations together. Our shared experience is abortion and often grief, but not always.

There is no hierarchy to abortion and there is no hierarchy to grief, but in society, there is a hierarchy around what we are allowed to grieve about publicly, such as the death of a parent or romantic partner. With abortion there is a pressure to put it in the corner, not just from people that are anti-abortion, but even from people who are pro-choice because they are like, "If you speak about the abortion grief, that fuels an anti-abortion argument, so you're not helping the movement." The same thinking limits people from the permission to wonder, without guilt, how their life would be different if they had not had an abortion. How old would this human be? What would they look like? We are not allowed to have those emotions. So yes, there is also the grief of not being able to fully emote in the way that feels natural around an abortion. Where are we able to grieve if the focus is legality?

Camille:

Yes. I think regularly about my unborn child. They would be turning five this summer, which is wild. In a parallel universe I am the parent of a five-year-old!

Can you say more about your thoughts around abortion as a legal issue?

Zachi:

I do not believe abortion should be a legal issue; the state should not be involved at all. Once you put abortion in this political pressure cooker, you leave no space for grief. Abortion is a form of healthcare and that should be the end of it. The work I am building community around is about changing the systems that we live in.

Camille:

Within late-stage capitalism, there's so little space to feel anything that reduces productivity, such as grief or mental health challenges. An example from the latest edition of the *Diagnostic and Statistical Manual of Mental Disorders (DSM)* is a new pathology called *prolonged grief disorder,* which refers to anyone that is grieving for more than six months to a year.[3] To me this shows how much effort there is to enforce states that facilitate productivity and pathologize emotions or states that get in the way of being an efficient worker. What are your thoughts on this?

Zachi:

This is why I hate the word *healing.* I hate it when people say, "I can help you heal from your abortion." Why do we need to heal? It is part of us. It can come up when it wants, and it does not mean that we are unwell or that the experience was bad. It is a human reaction. I should clarify, I think it is okay when people define for themselves something that feels healing, or if we each choose to heal from something, or find a tool helpful in our process. I just do not like it when people say someone else should be healed from certain experiences. This speaks to what you are saying about this pathologizing of grief or anything that renders us less productive. The push to heal or recover, even from other healthcare practitioners, often reinforces that you should not be feeling this. Or you should not be grieving after a certain amount of time. The word *healing* is often used in a dangerous way.

We see this being applied even to forms of bereavement that are deemed "okay" to grieve about such as losing a child or parent. How do you get over losing a child or a parent? I can imagine you can move through daily life, but why should there be a "getting over it"? It is a loss; it is okay for that to be part of your life.

Camille:

Yes, to grow around and with our loss.

Conversations around abortion can be incredibly binary and are often attached to the legal context alone. Most of the conversation revolves around whether it should be legal; or this moral-emotional component where if someone carries out their pregnancy, it is assumed that they love the baby. In contrast, if you have an abortion, it is assumed you do not have any feelings toward the baby at all. My experience was complex and full of shades of gray: I loved being pregnant, felt a connection to the being within me, and had a deep desire to be a parent.

Yet everything in my situation was telling me: I cannot do this right now. The elephant in the room for me was our economic system. I was afraid that I would struggle to meet my basic needs with a child, and be stigmatized for this, as I exist in a body that is commonly read as young, Black, and femme. Yet it is so rare that I hear people even mention economic considerations and access to resources when it comes to abortion. Part of my grief was realizing that if I lived in a different economic reality, I would have had a lot more choice. What are your thoughts about this?

Zachi:

Thank you for naming that. It is such a common factor. The approach we take at Dopo is from a standpoint of reproductive justice. The definition of *reproductive justice* is the right to have a child, not to have a child, and to raise the child or children we have in safe, healthy, and secure environments. Reproductive justice speaks to economic rights and access to education, it speaks to racial, migration, gender, and sexuality justice. It speaks to all these factors that are often ignored within the standard conversation of abortion when we focus on legality alone.

That is also why I say that I am pro-abortion because I am pro people having abortions if they want them or if they need them, but I am also for people being able to decide whether they want to parent or not. It is less about pro-choice because when people make decisions, they are not clean choices. If our society was a justice-based society, then we could talk about abortion as a choice. Again, not in all cases because sometimes abortion is necessary in situations beyond our control, and you do not have a choice if you want to remain alive and healthy.

As we do not live in a justice-based society, many areas of our complex, intersectional lives are not taken into consideration, so there are very few of us that have a choice when it comes to abortion. We make decisions around it—decisions that may feel like the best approaches for us.

Camille:

How does intersectionality relate to this?

Zachi:

If you move through the world as a young-looking, Black, AFAB pregnant person or parent, society often treats you as someone that is irresponsible. Sometimes stigma is put on you when you go to the abortion clinic, and they judge you for being "another one" that found yourself in this situation.

When the focus on abortion is legality, without looking at the criminalization system, wealth inequality, or how the police harm and frequently kill Black people, it ignores other real considerations people have about parenting. We are in a system that punishes you for being and for life happening to you. What type of society is that?

We must look at our education system and who has access to that. Who has access to housing? Who has access to citizenship in England today? We are learning in the UK that the government can take your citizenship away from you.[4] How is that a safe environment to make decisions that affect you and another human you would be caring for? Reproductive justice is a crucial part of social justice. It brings all these conversations together so we can envision what housing justice, support for parents, and economic rights could look like.

With the legal focus, the aim is to lower the number of abortions, but we should be focusing on housing or healthcare so people are not forced to make decisions they do not want to make in the first place. We do what is best for us within the contexts we find ourselves in.

Camille:

I feel that deeply. There is so much individualization of responsibility. The story we get is that abortion rates are increasing without exploring the systemic reasons that so many people are making that decision. What resources and support would folks need to have space for different outcomes? How does climate change impact this? I agree with you about how entangled reproductive justice is with most of the social questions we are holding at this moment in modernity.

When I look at what is happening in the US, with the right-wing attempts to reduce access to abortion, I am reminded of Silvia Federici's book *Caliban and the Witch.*[5] One of the main arguments is that the witch burning times were a tool used by the financial elite to increase the labor force after the Black Death by taking control of women's bodies and forcing them to reproduce. I sense that this is a similar attempt to produce more workers given that many Western nations have more elderly folks than young workers.

Zachi:

Yes, 100 percent! What a situation we find ourselves in . . .

Camille:

I trust we will collectively give it our best to change power dynamics and weave more care in our lifetimes.

I spent about five years actively processing my abortion grief and all the changes rippling in me that ricocheted from that. For example, during the first year, some early childhood trauma surfaced and that became a heavy knot to untangle. On the other side of this, I feel that the whole experience was an initiation process. In saying no to birthing another being, I was forced to rebirth myself, choose how to live, and discern what other things I wanted to grow.

That active agency and informed consent led to the embodied remembering of moments over many years in my childhood when my agency was taken away from me. Although this experience plunged me into some deep grief, it created the foundation for the life I am living right now, and I feel incredibly grateful for that. I also became aware of how afraid patriarchal systems are of women, AFAB, and femme folks being in our power.

I am wondering what comes up for you around this idea of abortion as initiation?

Zachi:

Thank you for sharing your experience, I also resonate with that. From my own experience and talking to other people, I now call abortion a revelatory experience. Once you have gone through it, it is as though you have pushed a reset button on life. It can make you question how you are going to live your life. Who are you going to be? It brings you to a point in your life where you cannot escape some truths about yourself.

It can push you to really live your life; to be the truest you have ever been to yourself, to your needs. It can stop you from denying yourself. It can allow you to face yourself in the beauty and the grief of past experiences. It can provide hope for the future. For me, my abortion was the experience that fundamentally changed the course of my whole life. I do not know what the alternative was, but I am now living a life that is truer to me, that has brought me in touch with myself and my body that I did not realize I was disconnected from before.

Since 2021, I have been working with an artist to create work around abortion, framing it as a rite of passage or ritual. We created a joint space for a few weeks called *Tracing Spaces* for people who had abortions during the pandemic. Each week for six weeks, we covered a different topic like remembering or releasing. I cannot remember all the topics, but it felt like an initiation that resonated with a lot of people. A person in the group shared, "This experience made me reevaluate my life and was a rebirth of my life. The longer I'm in this space, the more I reflect on my own experience." Another client of mine left their marriage because they realized they were only in a relationship with a man because of following the dominant trajectory of life that encourages people to be heterosexual, get married, and have kids. Their abortion led them to realize they are a wonderful queer being who deserves to live in all their glory. Many people have these experiences of abortion being a catalyst to living their deeper truth.

To me initiation, rebirth, rite of passage, or ritual are all wonderful connotations for abortion, and I dream of a world where people get to embrace this element of the process, rather than being steeped in fear or shame. That would change so many of us and our lives.

Camille:

Yes, allowing for expansion into full aliveness rather than shrinking, which is what most Western or "modern" societies seem to encourage. Complex feelings can be involved, but I love this vision of people stepping into abortion as a ritual experience, as a transformative life event. Something that can lead to more alignment, connection, and empowerment. This is what I want for people who make that decision.

Zachi:

I love that abortion can feature in our lives. The impact is not always simple or easy, but if we reframed it, talked about it differently, when people are younger and could remove it as a political hot potato, there would be less shame associated with it. Less put on us by society. It is a powerful experience.

Camille:

Yes. Everything you have spoken to shows me that there is so much of that power and nourishment that comes from being witnessed. I imagine it might be less easy to access this self-reflection and transformation if you have never spoken to anyone about it. If no one knows externally, perhaps there is less acknowledgment of its existence internally?

Zachi:

Of course, there is space for many different experiences, and I know there are truly people who feel that their abortions had no impact on their lives. Of the people who do say that, I believe there is a percentage of them who say that as a form of protection because they do not feel safe exploring the emotions of it. It is not a judgment because each of us must manage our lives.

The person I have supported with the longest distance between their abortion and speaking to anyone about it was fifteen years. We have also had people on the course in their sixties and their seventies who shared, "I had my abortion when I was eighteen and I worked in reproductive health, but in communications or human resources. Now in my older age, I can publicly say I had an abortion and I want to provide one-to-one support for other people that have gone through it." That silence, whether for forty years, fifteen years, or even five years, is a lot to carry. Of course, for many elders and people alive today in various parts of the world, it is an issue of safety on a personal, physical, or communal level. However, it is sad that something so big has not been able to be voiced.

Camille:

Yes, it is heartbreaking.

I am interested in how these legacies of secrecy, shame, and silence have been passed down. It is only for a few generations in many Western nations that people have been able to access abortion safely or legally, let alone speak about it. Perhaps the younger generations can be the turning point and we can actively talk to the children and young people in our lives about what abortion is so they are better prepared in case they make that decision. I never got information about it in school. Our sex education in general was not satisfactory.

Zachi:

Definitely not.

Camille:

I also want to uplift the ways that Dopo is holding space for trans and nonbinary kin having abortions. May more providers and health centers offer skillful, gender-expansive abortion care.

Zachi:

Some individual providers are trying, but generally it is rooted in the language of women's rights. From the advocacy movements to individual clinical or medical care, there is a long way to go, but like you said, we are moving. I keep reminding myself, we are moving, we are on our way, and we are part of a wider community, moving together and pushing forward.

Camille:

Thank you.

HOW TO USE THESE
GRIEF RITUALS

You are invited to create deliberate time and space to do these practices, even if you only have twenty minutes. Take the necessary steps to be present. This might include switching off your phone, the TV, or your computer as well as moving away from things that distract you. For example, ensuring that kids or pets in your life can be in a separate space. I suggest that you open each ritual with one of the embodiment tools outlined in the following pages to connect with your body and get a sense of how you are feeling. These practices incorporate touch and breath while using your awareness to track sensation in your body.

Once you are present, I invite you to feel into your intention or the memory you would like to work with. Allow this to be in your consciousness as you do the grief ritual. Once you feel satisfied and ready to end your ritual, I suggest finishing with one of the integration practices outlined in the "Integration Practices" section later on to close. These can help you reflect on and emotionally digest your experience whilst giving a signal to your body that it is time to shift into another space.

The framework for these grief rituals is rooted in the belief that grief work is generative, but due to grief tending being suppressed in the Western context, it can sometimes be overwhelming. You are encouraged to stay with your embodied experience as much as possible during the rituals. If you notice you are becoming overwhelmed or disconnected, I invite you to pause, take a break, or use an embodiment tool to reconnect to your body if this feels supportive. Please be gentle with yourself.

Feel free to use any additional support to make yourself comfortable while using these rituals such as burning incense, listening to music, or wearing comfortable clothing. If you would like to make adaptations, please follow what is most nourishing and generative for you.

Using the Embodiment Practices

The embodiment tools outlined here are rooted in the Resilience Toolkit, created by Nkem Ndefo. I am a certified instructor for the Resilience Toolkit and have consent to integrate these tools and the framework alongside the following grief rituals.

Please note that in this context, the Resilience Toolkit is intended for personal and peer use. In order to keep people safe, please do not formally teach these practices or use them for commercial gain unless you have been certified in the Resilience Toolkit via Lumos Transforms. Despite the simplicity of the practices, there is nuance and skill required to facilitate these safely with others.

If you are interested in training, further facilitation, or guidance in the Resilience Toolkit, please visit www.lumostransforms.com.

Please be aware that not all the practices may work for your body. When you try a new practice, please track your sensations to determine if a specific tool is helpful at that moment. If you are doing a practice and feel tension or discomfort, please stop. However, if a tool is creating sensations in your body that are grounding, nourishing, or reducing stress, please notice what signals your body is giving you that show that it feels supportive. Some examples might include your belly softening, your breath deepening, or your thoughts becoming calmer.

If you notice that it is hard to feel many sensations, do not worry. It can take time to reconnect to sensation and these signals may be small at first. As Staci Haines notes,

> Since many of us have needed to turn away from our sensations because of trauma and oppression, or have been trained out of paying attention to them, here are some things you can pay attention to, to feel more of them: temperatures—more warm or more cool; movement—pulsing (heart, pulses), breath (in and out), tingling, streaming, twitching; and pressure—places you feel more contracted and places you feel more relaxed. When you notice your sensations try and be inside of them, rather than being an outside observer.[1]

As you try these embodiment practices, I invite you to track whether a particular one creates a noticeable sensation of grounding or stress reduction in your body. I suggest that you use this practice or another that you have identified as helpful as your initial embodiment practice at the start of a grief ritual.

As we tend to grief over time using these rituals and embodiment practices, the aim is to avoid overwhelm and cultivate the capacity to be with bigger sensations when it is adaptive for us.

Begin a grief ritual with one of the following embodiment practices. Please note that the embodiment practices are all designed to be used in a short amount of time, ideally two minutes each, with the exception of *Resourcing* which can take closer to five minutes.

BUTTERFLY HUG

1. Lift your hands in front of you so the palms are facing your chest.

2. Cross your hands over each other in front of your body.

3. Place your hands on your chest near your collarbone.

4. Tap your hands rhythmically at the pace and pressure that feel best to your body.

5. Notice the sensations in your body as you do this.

* If you feel tension or discomfort during this practice please stop.

* If you notice that this practice feels grounding or nourishing in some way, notice what signals your body is giving you that demonstrate this.

KNEE TAPPING

1. Extend your arms out in front of your body and cross one over the other, palms facing down.

2. Allow your hands to meet your knees or touch somewhere on your thighs.

3. Tap your hands on your knees or thighs at the pace and pressure that feel good to you.

4. Notice the sensations in your body as you do this.

* If you feel tension or discomfort during this practice please stop.
* If you notice that this practice feels grounding or nourishing in some way, notice what signals your body is giving you that demonstrate this.

ORIENTING

1. Begin by slowly moving your head and neck in a circular motion to take in the space around you. Allow your eyes to widen as you notice the space you are in.

2. Notice any colors or objects that stand out to you.

3. Notice any smells you can smell.

4. Notice the sensation of your clothing against your skin.

* If you feel tension or discomfort during this practice please stop.
* If you notice that this practice feels grounding or nourishing in some way, notice what signals your body is giving you that demonstrate this.

RESOURCING

1. Begin by getting comfortable in a seated position.

2. Notice any points of connection between your body and the floor or your body and your chair.

3. Notice any sensations arising in your body as you breathe.

4. Scan your body and find the place that feels most pleasant, without you having to do anything to it. If you are experiencing physical pain, the invitation is to find a place in your body that feels neutral.

5. Focus on this place for a few moments, noticing any ripples or shifts in sensation.

* If you feel tension or discomfort during this practice please stop.

* If you notice that this practice feels grounding or nourishing in some way, notice what signals your body is giving you that demonstrate this.

HAND ON CHEST AND BELLY

1. Place one hand on your chest and another on your belly if this feels good.

2. Notice the warmth arising from these points of connection on your body.

3. Notice any sensations that arise in your body.

* If you feel tension or discomfort during this practice please stop.
* If you notice that this practice feels grounding or nourishing in some way, notice what signals your body is giving you that demonstrate this.

HEAD HOLD

1. Place a hand on your forehead and the other on the back of your head or neck.

2. Notice the warmth arising from these points of connection on your body.

3. Notice any other sensations that arise in your body.

* If you feel tension or discomfort during this practice please stop.
* If you notice that this practice feels grounding or nourishing in some way, notice what signals your body is giving you that demonstrate this.

Personal Grief Rituals

These rituals can be done alone to tend grief in your daily life. Most can be experienced in as little as twenty minutes but can be extended as needed. Feel free to experiment and find what works best for you.

ALTAR PRACTICE

If you have specific ancestors you would like to honor or be in conversation with about your grief or the events in your life, consider setting up an altar for them in your home. The following is one approach you can take to set up an ancestor altar and develop a regular relationship with them.

In daily life or in times of transition, it can be grounding to meditate near your altar, speak with your ancestors, and light a candle for them regularly.

For your altar, you will need the following supplies:

- A box, shelf, or side table to function as the altar structure

- A white cloth

- Photos of the ancestors you wish to honor

- A large, white candle

- Incense if desired

- Two small vessels or cups

- If your ancestors liked alcohol, alcohol of their choice; gin, for example

- Flowers or a small living plant

- Other sacred objects of your choosing

When you are ready to construct your altar, follow these steps:

1. Find a place in your home for the altar.

2. Place the white cloth on the altar structure so the surface is covered.

3. Place the photos on the wall above the altar or on the structure.

4. Place the candle or incense in a central location.

5. Fill one of the vessels with water and add it to the structure.

6. Fill the other with alcohol your ancestors liked.

7. Add flowers or a living plant.

8. Add any other sacred objects.

9. Once all items are where you want them, speak your intention for this altar and the relationship you would like with your ancestors. Light the candle or incense. Thank your ancestors. Tend to your altar regularly.

THE GRIEF JAR

This ritual comes from Tricia Hersey of the Nap Ministry and has been adapted slightly.

You will need the following:

- A jar with a lid
- A piece of scrap paper, cut into small bits, large enough to write a few sentences on
- A pen
- A large bowl
- Water or a small candle

When you are ready to begin:

1. Place your jar on your altar or somewhere in your home that you see regularly.

2. Place the pieces of paper next to the jar. Place a pen here too.

3. When you feel a moment of grief or sorrow moving in you, write it down on one of the small pieces of paper and place it in the jar.

4. On the full moon or new moon, make a ritual to release the grief that has built up in your jar.

There are two options for this ritual:

OPTION 1

    a. Fill a large bowl or vessel with water.

    b. Use an embodiment practice of your choice.

c. Take time to reflect on each moment of grief written on the pieces of paper in your jar. Remove one piece and release any sounds, tears, or words that feel necessary.

d. When you are ready, release the bit of paper into the water allowing it to submerge.

e. Repeat until you have emptied the contents of your jar.

OPTION 2: AN ALTERNATIVE WITH FIRE

a. Place a small candle into a large bowl or vessel.

b. Use an embodiment practice of your choice.

c. Take time to reflect on each moment of grief written on a piece of paper. Release any sounds, tears, or words that feel necessary.

d. When you are ready, release the paper into the candle flame allowing it to burn.

e. Repeat until you have emptied your jar.

This can also be done with an outdoor fire or fireplace. Take care to do this safely if you choose to work with fire.

5. Once your moon ritual is complete, return your jar to its place and restock your paper next to it.

DANCE YOUR GRIEF

This ritual is something I have been doing for the last few years. It is inspired by my Yoruba ancestors who used dance as a healing tool. You will need the following:

- A playlist, mix, or selection of music that will support you in releasing your grief. I recommend at least fifteen minutes of music, if not more. An hour session is ideal.
- Speakers or headphones with rich bass frequencies
- A space to dance where you feel comfortable and have as much privacy as you need

When you are ready to practice:

1. Begin with an embodiment practice of your choice.

2. Ask your body, Where am I holding grief? What do I need to do to release it?

3. Put the music on.

4. Move in a way that best serves your intention and is based on the desires of your body.

5. Allow sounds, moaning, or tears to flow as you dance with your grief.

6. When you are ready to close, give yourself some moments to connect with your body, to thank yourself.

7. If you have time, integrate your experience and anything you noticed during the grief dance by journaling, drawing, or meditating for ten minutes or longer.

STONES RITUAL

This ritual is adapted from *The Wild Edge of Sorrow: Rituals of Renewal and the Sacred Work of Grief* by Francis Weller.[2]

You will need the following:

- A bucket, soup pot, or large bowl filled with water
- Several stones and pebbles. I'd suggest ten to fifteen, but use more if you need to.

When you are ready:

1. Set up your space in a way that is pleasing to you.

2. Begin by doing an embodiment practice.

3. Set an intention or notice what you would like to grieve.

4. Take a stone in your hands and allow your grief to pour into it. It helps to work with specific moments or memories.

5. Allow yourself to release for as long as you need to. This may be with words, or by crying, rocking, or engaging with some other embodiment that feels right for you.

6. Allow the stone to drop into the water when you are ready to let go.

7. Repeat this process until you have run out of stones.

8. Thank yourself and use an integration practice to close.

PILLOW SCREAMING

You will need the following:

- A pillow
- A space where you feel comfortable with as much privacy as you desire
- A mat or cushions to support your body to be as comfortable as possible

When you are ready:

1. Begin with an embodiment practice to ground yourself.

   If you feel overwhelmed during the ritual, please pause, or use an embodiment practice if you would like to ground yourself and return to the ritual.

2. Set an intention or notice what memory or grief you would like to work with.

3. Find a comfortable position.

4. Scream or moan into your pillow in the way that feels best for your body.

   You can also punch or hit your pillow if that feels good. Be sure to take care of your voice. It can be helpful to scream or moan at a lower pitch as high-pitched screaming can hurt your throat.

5. Do this for up to twenty minutes and then take a break to check in with your body and your needs.

6. Finish with an integration practice.

ABORTION RITUAL: VISUALIZATION MEDITATION

This ritual is a visualization meditation that can be useful for people who wish to connect with the being they are carrying before a termination. This practice was shared with me by the partner I was pregnant with.

You will need the following:

- A space you feel comfortable in
- A candle

When you are ready:

1. Set up your space in a way that is pleasing to you.
2. Begin with an embodiment practice.
3. Set your intention.
4. Light the candle.
5. Close your eyes if that feels comfortable, or gently rest your gaze somewhere in your space.
6. Scan your body and find the place that feels most pleasant.
7. Focus on this place in your body for a few moments. Know that you can always return here if you feel overwhelmed.
8. Visualize a vast lake in front of you.
9. Visualize yourself at the shore with a little rowboat.
10. Step into the boat and row towards the middle of the lake.
11. Visualize your unborn child at the center of the lake in a boat of their own.

12. Meet your unborn child and share anything you need to with them. This might be why you are not ready or able to birth them. Take as much time as you need for this.

13. When you have shared everything you need to and you have released any tears that arise, ask them with love to turn back towards the spirit realm in their boat.

14. Visualize turning your boat around and rowing back to the shore.

15. Open your eyes when you are ready.

16. Thank yourself and do an integration practice.

SHRINE FOR AN UNBORN BABY

You may wish to make a small altar or shrine for your unborn; by doing so, you can create a space to honor them or grieve for them in your healing process.

What you will need:

- An old sewing box, or a piece of cardboard, or something that will serve as the base for your shrine
- Your ultrasound photos
- Paint or any materials to decorate

When you are ready:

1. Begin with an embodiment practice.

2. Decorate your box or shrine in the way that feels most pleasing to you. If you would like, you can include the photos of your pregnancy scans, paintings, collages. Anything that will help you to remember this being. You could also choose to include a name if you did a naming ritual for them.

3. Once your shrine is ready, place it somewhere in your home.

4. When you feel called, you can place candles by it or do grief rituals near it.

MOANING AND ROCKING

This can be used on its own as a practice or during any of the other grief rituals. Both moaning and rocking can support grief to flow.

What you will need:

- A space in which you feel at ease
- Pillows or a mat to ensure your body is comfortable

When you are ready:

1. Begin with an embodiment practice.

2. Set your intention about what you would like to grieve.

3. Rock your body at the rhythm and pace that feels best to you.

4. Add in low moaning if desired.

5. Do this for as long as it feels supportive.

6. Finish with an integration practice.

Community Grief Rituals

SHARING CIRCLE

This is a simple yet powerful way for people to share grief in a group context. It is best done in pairs or groups of three or more.

Before you start:

- Decide on the amount of time you will hold space for each other. For example, you might choose to close after one hour or after everyone has shared three times.

- If it feels useful, find an object to use as a talking stick.

- Decide on any ground rules or shared agreements: for example, confidentiality, not interrupting each other, not giving advice unless requested, or other rules that feel supportive.

When you are ready:

1. Sit in a circle and get comfortable.

2. Begin by doing an embodiment practice.

3. Take turns passing the talking object and sharing any grief that is moving for you. Allow tears or sounds to flow as needed.

4. When other people are sharing, give them attention by focusing on their words and deeply listening without interruption.

5. Close with an integration practice.

CANDLE VIGIL

Use this practice to honor someone who has died or to commemorate a collective event that needs to be grieved. Vigils can be intimate affairs as well as a template for mass actions or demonstrations.[3]

You will need:

- A candle per person

- Images of the person who has died or the event to be grieved

- A group of people gathering in person or online

- One or more people to facilitate

When you are ready:

1. Welcome the group and frame the purpose or intention of the event.

2. Begin with an embodiment practice if that feels supportive.

3. Each participant lights their candle and shares memories of the person who has died. Release stories, words, and tears as needed.

4. If your vigil is part of a demonstration or march, you might like to walk with lit candles and images and then share memories or speeches at a set destination at the end.

5. When everyone has finished sharing, use an integration practice to finish.

WATER POURING RITUAL

This ritual was shown to me by Marika Heinrichs, a somatic practitioner, during a session we cofacilitated. Marika's inspiration for this practice includes a libations grief practice held by adrienne maree brown at Allied Media Conference[4] as well as by Celtic and Germanic water offerings.

Before you begin:

- Decide on the amount of time you will hold space for each other. For example, you might choose to close after one hour or after everyone has shared three times.

- Decide on any ground rules or shared agreements: i.e., confidentiality, not interrupting each other, not giving advice unless requested, or other rules that feel aligned.

- Make sure each person has two vessels: an empty vessel and another holding water that will be poured into the empty vessel.

When you are ready:

1. Assemble your group in person or online.

2. Begin by framing your ritual or giving an intention.

3. Do an embodiment practice.

4. Invite each person to share some aspect of grief that they are working with. When they share, invite everyone else in the group to pour some water into their empty vessel.

5. Repeat until all the water is gone or until you reach the end of the time for which you have agreed to hold the space.

6. Remember to pause or take time to resource and ground so you can stay connected to your body.

7. Share reflections and close with an integration practice.

A GRIEF DATE WITH THE FOREST OR OCEAN

This practice is adapted from *The Smell of Rain on Dust: Grief and Praise* by Martín Prechtel.[5]

Before you begin:

- Select a place to go to: a forest or the sea.

- Choose a friend to accompany you. Ensure that they have the capacity to allow you to release without trying to soothe you or minimize your emotions. Their role is to be a physical companion to you and offer you support if you need it.

When you are ready:

1. Begin with an embodiment practice.

2. Set your intention.

3. Find a place to sit near the sea or in the forest, accompanied by your friend for support.

4. Vocalize your grief. Speak, sing, moan, or cry as much as you need to and allow yourself to notice how it feels to be witnessed and supported by your friend, as well as by the sea or the forest.

5. Do this for as long as it feels supportive.

6. Close with an integration practice.

PEER SUPPORT: HOLDING PRACTICES

These holding practices can be helpful for someone who is grieving and in need of physical support. The most important thing is to ensure that you have consent before engaging in touch so please make sure that you have received that from the person needing support.

What you will need:

- A person to work with

- Pillows or other supports, such as a sofa, that enable you to both be comfortable

- A space where you can be vulnerable without being self-conscious

When you are ready, ask the grieving person what kind of touch they would like:

CHEST SUPPORT

1. Ask if you can place a hand on the grieving person's chest.

2. Let them guide you to where it is comfortable for their body.

3. Leave your hand there while they share or cry. I recommend keeping your hand still as this can provide grounding presence rather than moving which can signal to the person that they need to stop crying.

4. Remove your hand when they are ready.

BACK SUPPORT

1. Ask if you can place a hand on the grieving person's back.

2. Let them guide you to where it is comfortable for their body.

3. Leave your hand there while they share or cry. I recommend keeping your hand still as this can provide grounding presence rather than moving which can signal to the person that they need to stop crying.

4. Remove your hand when they are ready.

RECLINING SUPPORT

1. Ask the grieving person if they would like to be held and allow them to lean back against you so their back is being supported by your chest.

2. Make sure that both of you are comfortable. It can be helpful for the support person to be propped up against a sofa or cushions against a wall.

3. Support their body while they share, cry, or release.

GIVE IT TO THE FIRE

What you will need:

- An indoor fireplace or wood burner with a lit fire; alternatively, an outdoor fire
- A group of people
- Paper and pens
- Other objects to burn

When you are ready:

1. Begin with an embodiment practice.

2. Set the intention for the fire: to process grief, to let go, or whatever feels aligned for you.

3. Ask people to gather around.

4. Invite people to write down what they wish to grieve or let go of on pieces of paper.

5. Take turns offering things to the fire. As you do this, you can share any words, tears, or sounds that feel supportive.

6. If it is supportive, use an integration practice to end this ritual.

Integration Practices

When you are finishing a grief ritual, it can be helpful to do a practice to begin digesting what has taken place emotionally. This can include thanking ancestors or elements that helped to support your grief tending. It can also involve sharing gratitude, using touch as well as verbal or written processing. This signals that it is time to appreciate what took place and transition into another moment.

The following practices are a few examples of what you can do to close a ritual. If you enjoy using other tools, please work with what is most helpful for you.

GIVE IT TO THE EARTH

This practice was shared with me by Farzana Khan of Healing Justice London during the grief retreat we facilitated.

1. Take a moment to sense your body and notice what is arising.

2. Sitting down or standing, sweep your hands down your body (or a few inches in front of your body) from your face all the way down to your feet, visualizing any residual energy that needs to be cleared, returning it to the earth where it can be regenerated.

3. When you arrive at your feet, allow your hands to connect with the earth for as long as this feels good.

4. Repeat three times or for as long as you desire.

GRATITUDE

1. Place your hands on some parts of your body that feel comfortable; this could be a hand on your chest and a hand on your belly.

2. Take a few moments to notice any sensations arising for you.

3. Notice the warmth from your hands as they connect to your body.

4. Visualize sending gratitude through your hands—you might like to imagine golden light entering through your skin and rippling through your form.

5. Thank your ancestors, or other spiritual support, for helping you to be with your grief.

6. Thank yourself for taking the time to tend your grief.

7. Stay with this for a couple of minutes or as long as it feels good for you.

WRITTEN REFLECTIONS

Take a few moments to write down anything that feels important to release or remember. Feel free to use a stream-of-consciousness approach where you do not pay too much attention to grammar or whether it makes perfect sense to others.

VERBAL REFLECTIONS—GROUP

Invite each participant to share something that was meaningful for them about the experience of the ritual.

JOURNAL QUESTIONS

These questions are intended to help you explore your relationship to grief and notice what would be supportive as you befriend your grief. Feel free to reflect on them via journaling or another contemplative practice such as meditation or collaging.

- How can I befriend my grief?

- How was grief or loss addressed within my family or by the people who raised me?

- What community support does my heart long for when I am grieving?

- What ancestral practices or customs did my ancestors have to navigate grief or loss?

- How does my unaddressed grief make itself known in my body or daily life?

- What emotions are easier for me to access, and which ones are harder to feel?

- What past experiences long for permission to be felt?

- What does my grief teach me about what I love or what is most precious in my life?

HERBAL MEDICINE
FOR GRIEF

Plant companions in the form of herbal teas have been instrumental in supporting me to navigate chronic health issues during my life, to soothe inflammation and create ease in my body. During my grief awakening, I also relied upon plant companions to support me. The following are some of the teas I found most supportive during this time. When making the teas, you only need a small pinch of each herb. Allow them to steep for at least five minutes. I recommend using a tea pot or strainer.

- To relieve anxiety: Skullcap | Passionflower

- To support sleep, induce drowsiness: Chamomile | Valerian | Lavender

- To support the heart and energy levels: Hawthorn | Motherwort

- To recover from sexual trauma: Damiana

- To support the nervous system: Licorice | Nettle | Reishi Mushroom (capsules/tincture) | Lion's Mane Mushroom (capsules/tincture) | Tulsi

- To support womb recovery after miscarriage/abortion: *Combine and cover with boiling water, steep for at least six minutes:* Raspberry Leaf, Nettle, Yarrow, Dandelion, Oatstraw. *Drink daily for at least two weeks.*

- To support the immune system: *Combine one teaspoon of each and boil in a cooking pot for 20 minutes:* Ginger root, Turmeric root, Black pepper, Thyme, Coltsfoot, Elderberries, and Garlic. *Add lemon juice if desired.*

It is possible to source loose leaf herbs for tea at apothecaries such as Neal's Yard in the UK or from various retailers online including health food shops.

Please note that I am not a medical practitioner and cannot give official medical advice. Please consult an herbalist, doctor, or medical practitioner before use.

CLOSING THOUGHTS

I hope that this book is supportive for you and the communities you are connected to. It has been a deep journey to research and compile this over the last years. I have waded through the last tendrils of my own abortion grief, relived my history of childhood sexual abuse, supported my partner through the death of a parent, engaged in family mediation work, and navigated the various challenges related to existing during a pandemic. It has been quite intense at times. I am so grateful to my ancestors, friends, and community of care who have supported me to complete this project so it can continue its life in the world.

In my wild visions for this book and how it may ripple into the world in years to come, I imagine regular grief rituals being incorporated into movements for social change, as well as other networks, as practices of care and interdependence. Everyone will be encouraged to attend monthly grief rituals as an entry point for organizing work. Communal weeping and emotional release will become normalized, held with the knowledge that this release allows us to compost our feelings and make space for more presence to show up, to be flexible in our thinking, and to operate in ways that feel aligned with our values. These grief spaces will enable us to make generative connections between our own lives, our ancestors, and the stories of the lands we inhabit or are ancestrally connected to. We will all have space in the community to be with our sorrow and be embraced with tenderness. As a first step towards this vision, I hope that we as activists, changemakers, parents, caregivers, healers, and artists will be courageous enough to give regular grief tending a chance and then learn to hold space for this in our lives and within our communities.

Despite believing in the importance of grief work, I encounter resistance towards it from time to time. I am still learning to make regular space for grief in my life outside of crisis moments. Thankfully, when grief arises in me, I am learning to ride the waves with more ease and trust than I used to. I sense that learning to be with my grief will be a lifelong process of repatterning old ways of being and consciously practicing what I would like to embody. Rather than seeing myself as an expert, I see myself as engaged and in the early parts of my journey with grief work. My intention is to commit to the habit of a monthly grief ritual to support my well-being and presence. This is inspired by the Dagara approach and the work of Sobonfu and Malidoma Somé, which has been pivotal to this project. In the years to come, I would like to cultivate space in my local community to practice grief rituals on a regular basis.

I feel confident in the need to hold grief work in peer networks, rather than outsourcing it to a small group of paid professionals. Many therapists who work with grief in the Western context prioritize helping people to "move on" so they can become "productive" members of society again, rather than supporting them to see grief as a generative force.

What if we were resourced enough to support our friends, peers, and loved ones when they were grieving? How would that increase our bonds of intimacy, of trust? Our sense of collective care and interdependence? I wonder if collective grief tending will allow us to embody innovative ideas and experiment, to grow the more beautiful world our hearts know is possible.

I hope that this book creates ripples of compassion, trust, vulnerability, and ease. Ultimately, I hope it supports life-sustaining practices for the next seven generations to come.

With love and solidarity,

Camille Sapara Barton

FURTHER READING

- *The Spirit of Intimacy: Ancient African Teachings in the Ways of Relationships* by Sobonfu Somé
- *The Healing Wisdom of Africa: Finding Life Purpose Through Nature, Ritual, and Community* by Malidoma Patrice Somé
- *The Wild Edge of Sorrow: Rituals of Renewal and the Sacred Work of Grief* by Francis Weller
- *Die Wise: A Manifesto for Sanity and Soul* by Stephen Jenkinson
- *The Smell of Rain on Dust: Grief and Praise* by Martín Prechtel
- *Rebellious Mourning: The Collective Work of Grief* by Cindy Milstein
- *Climate: A New Story* by Charles Eisenstein
- *Grieving While Black: An Antiracist Take on Oppression and Sorrow* by Breeshia Wade
- *Finding Meaning: The Sixth Stage of Grief* by David Kessler
- *Dancing Wisdom: Embodied Knowledge in Haitian Vodou, Cuban Yoruba, and Bahian Candomblé* by Yvonne Daniel
- *Love and Rage: The Path of Liberation Through Anger* by Lama Rod Owens
- *Grievers* by adrienne maree brown
- *Healing Justice Lineages: Dreaming at the Crossroads of Liberation, Collective Care, and Safety* by Cara Page and Erica Woodland
- *In the Wake: On Blackness and Being* by Christina Sharpe

NOTES

Introduction

1 Mariame Kaba, *We Do This 'Til We Free Us: Abolitionist Organizing and Transforming Justice* (Chicago: Haymarket Books, 2021), 20.

2 Malkia Devich-Cyril, "Grief Belongs in Social Movements. Can We Embrace It?," *In These Times*, July 28, 2021, https://inthesetimes.com/article/freedom-grief-healing-death-liberation-movements.

3 *Repatterning* is my preferred term instead of healing. I first heard this term from Nkem Ndefo of Lumos Transforms. I like that it speaks to changing the patterns that keep us stuck in behaviors that harm ourselves or others.

4 Ecologies of Transformation (2021–2023) was a temporary master's program, curated and directed by Camille Sapara Barton at Sandberg Institute. The course explored how art-making and embodiment can create social change. To learn more visit www.ecologiesoftransformation.com.

5 Robin Wall Kimmerer, *Braiding Sweetgrass: Indigenous Wisdom, Scientific Knowledge, and the Teachings of Plants* (London: Penguin Books, 2020), 328.

6 The phrase *seven generations to come* relates to Haudenosaunee Confederacy philosophy that the choices we make in the present should take into account the wellbeing of those who will exist seven generations from now.

The Ongoing Grief of Colonization

1 Rupa Marya and Raj Patel, *Inflamed: Deep Medicine and the Anatomy of Injustice* (London: Allen Lane, 2021), 14–15.

2 Christina Sharpe, *In the Wake: On Blackness and Being* (London: Duke University Press, 2016).

3 Meron Moges-Gerbi, "Ralph Yarl, Teen Shot after Ringing Wrong Doorbell, Attends Brain Injury Event on Memorial Day," *CNN,* May 30, 2023, https://edition.cnn.com/2023/05/30/us/kansas-city-wrong -doorbell-shooting/index.html; Dake Kang, "Officer Who Shot Tamir Rice in 2014 Fired by the City of Cleveland," *PBS,* May 30, 2017, https: //www.pbs.org/newshour/politics/officer-shot-tamir-rice-2014-fired -cleveland-police; Siddharth Kara, "Is Your Phone Tainted by the Misery of the 35,000 Children in Congo's Mines?," *Guardian,* October 12, 2018, www.theguardian.com/global-development/2018/oct/12 /phone-misery-children-congo-cobalt-mines-drc.

4 *Global majority* is an umbrella term that refers to African heritage people, Asian heritage people, as well as those who are indigenous to various lands. This term seeks to highlight that people who exist outside of the white identity are the majority of the global population. This is in contrast to the ways that Black, Asian, and Indigenous people are often labelled as minorities within many Western contexts.

5 "Count Me in 2010," *National Mental Health Development Unit,* April 2011, www.mentalhealthlaw.co.uk/media/CQC_Count_me_in_2010.pdf.

6 The National Health Service (NHS) has provided free healthcare to people living in the UK since the 1960s. This has been a huge support for all people, along with the system of social welfare, and this has led to the impact of inequality being reduced in the UK.

7 *Conditioned tendencies* is a term popularized by Richard Strozzi-Heckler which refers to the automatic responses we have to stimuli which keep us operating in the same way, often feeling as though we don't have other choices.

8 Martín Prechtel, *The Smell of Rain on Dust: Grief and Praise* (Berkeley, CA: North Atlantic Books, 2015).

9 Sobonfu Somé, "Embracing Grief," Spirit Rock, accessed July 7, 2023, www.spiritrock.org/2016/the-teachings/article-archive/article-embracing -grief.

10 Mark Fisher, *Capitalist Realism: Is There No Alternative?* (Winchester, Hampshire, UK: Zero Books, 2009).

11 adrienne maree brown, *Emergent Strategy: Shaping Change, Changing Worlds* (Chico, CA: AK Press, 2017).

12 Tricia Hersey, *Rest Is Resistance: Free Yourself from Grind Culture and Reclaim Your Life* (London: Aster, 2022).

13 Oyèrónké Oyewùmi, *The Invention of Women: Making an African Sense of Western Gender Discourses* (Minneapolis: University of Minnesota Press, 1997); Caleb Okereke, "How U.S. Evangelicals Helped Homophobia Flourish in Africa," *Foreign Policy*, March 19, 2023, https://foreignpolicy.com/2023/03/19/africa-uganda-evangelicals -homophobia-antigay-bill/.

14 *One tongue* is a term for the English language used by Bayo Akomolafe in his book *These Wilds Beyond Our Fences: Letters to My Daughter on Humanity's Search for Home* (Berkeley, CA: North Atlantic Books, 2017).

15 Marya and Patel, *Inflamed*, 61.

16 Audre Lorde, *Sister Outsider: Essays and Speeches by Audre Lorde* (Berkeley, CA: Crossing Press, 2007).

17 Hersey, *Rest Is Resistance*.

18 Arundhati Roy, "The Pandemic Is a Portal," *Financial Times,* April 3, 2020, www.ft.com/content/10d8f5e8-74eb-11ea-95fe-fcd274e920ca.

19 Robert Booth and Caelainn Barr, "Black People Four Times More Likely to Die from Covid-19, ONS Finds," *Guardian,* May 7, 2020, www.theguardian.com/world/2020/may/07/black-people-four -times-more-likely-to-die-from-covid-19-ons-finds; Ed Pilkington, "Black Americans Dying of Covid-19 at Three Times the Rate of

White People," *Guardian,* May 20, 2020, www.theguardian.com/world
/2020/may/20/black-americans-death-rate-covid-19-coronavirus.

20 Marya and Patel, *Inflamed,* 10.

21 NHS Workforce, "Ethnicity Facts and Figures," *Gov.UK,* www.ethnicity
-facts-figures.service.gov.uk/workforce-and-business/workforce
-diversity/nhs-workforce/latest.

22 A. Kapilashrami et al., "Ethnic Disparities in Health & Social Care
Workers' Exposure, Protection, and Clinical Management of the
COVID-19 Pandemic in the UK," *Critical Public Health* 32, no. 1
(2022): 68–81.

23 "Written Evidence Submitted by Aston University," *UK Parliament
Committees*, April 2020, accessed July 10, 2023, https://committees
.parliament.uk/writtenevidence/2948/html/.

24 OECD, "The Unequal Impact of COVID-19: A Spotlight on Frontline Workers, Migrants and Racial/Ethnic Minorities," *OECD Policy
Responses to Corona Virus,* March 17, 2022, www.oecd.org/coronavirus
/policy-responses/the-unequal-impact-of-covid-19-a-spotlight-on
-frontline-workers-migrants-and-racial-ethnic-minorities-f36e931e/.

25 "UK Hostile Compensation Scheme Fails Windrush Victims," *Human
Rights Watch,* April 17, 2023, www.hrw.org/news/2023/04/17/uk-hostile
-compensation-scheme-fails-windrush-victims.

26 Philipa Roxby, "Record Alcohol Deaths from Pandemic Drinking,"
BBC, December 8, 2022, www.bbc.com/news/health-63902852.

27 *Release,* "Drugs in the Time of COVID: Interim Report," accessed
July 10, 2023, www.release.org.uk/publications/covid-drugs-market
-survey.

28 See the research that MAPS has been doing: https://maps.org/our
-research/.

29 Harriet Washington, *Medical Apartheid: The Dark History of Medical
Experimentation on Black Americans from Colonial Times to the Present*
(New York: Anchor, 2008).

30 Timothy Michaels, Jennifer Purdon, Alexis Collins, and Monnica Williams, "Inclusion of People of Color in Psychedelic-Assisted Psychotherapy: A Review of the Literature," *BMC Psychiatry* 18, no. 245 (2018).

31 Jack Patrick Hayes, "The Opium Wars in China," *Asia Pacific Curriculum,* accessed July 10, 2023, https://asiapacificcurriculum.ca/learning -module/opium-wars-china#.

32 Neil Woods and J. S. Rafaeli, *Drug Wars: The Real Inside Story of Britain's Drug War* (London: Ebury Press, 2018), 19–22.

33 Kojo Koram, *The War on Drugs and the Global Colour Line* (London: Pluto Press, 2019).

34 Camille Barton and Imani Robinson, "Drug Policy and the Fight for Black Lives," *Vice,* November 2, 2017, www.vice.com/en/article/ne33yw /drug-policy-and-the-fight-for-black-lives.

35 *Release, The Colour of Injustice: 'Race,' Drugs and Law Enforcement in England and Wales,* accessed July 10, 2023, www.release.org.uk /publications/ColourOfInjustice.

36 *Release,* "Drugs in the Time of COVID."

37 *Release, The Colour of Injustice.*

38 Marcus Biddle, "Understanding the Mental Health Impact of Stop and Frisk and Frequent Police Stops," *WHYY PBS,* December 5, 2022, https://whyy.org/articles/stop-and-frisk-philadelphia-mental -health-implications/; Jordan E. DeVylder, Courtney Cogburn, Hans Y. Oh, Deidre Anglin, Melissa Edmondson Smith, Tanya Sharpe, Hyun-Jin Jun, Jason Schiffman, Ellen Lukens, and Bruce Link, "Psychotic Experiences in the Context of Police Victimization: Data from the Survey of Police—Public Encounters," *Schizophrenia Bulletin: The Journal of Psychoses and Related Disorders* 43, no. 5 (September 2017): 993–1001.

39 Written evidence submitted by Black Mental Health UK, *UK Parliament,* January 2013, https://publications.parliament.uk/pa/cm201213 /cmselect/cmhaff/494/494we06.htm.

40 BAME Deaths in Police Custody, *Inquest,* www.inquest.org.uk/bame
-deaths-in-police-custody; written evidence submitted by Black
Mental Health UK.

41 Sophie K Rosa, *Radical Intimacy* (London: Pluto Press, 2023), 29.

42 Jonathan Metzl, *The Protest Psychosis: How Schizophrenia Became a
Black Disease* (Boston: Beacon Press, 2011).

43 Michelle Alexander, *The New Jim Crow: Mass Incarceration in the Age of
Colorblindness* (New York: The New Press, 2012).

44 *Release,* "Regulating Right, Repairing Wrongs: Exploring Equity and
Social Justice Initiatives within UK Cannabis Reform," accessed July 10,
2023, www.release.org.uk/publications/cannabis-regulating-right.

45 Kimmerer, *Braiding Sweetgrass,* 328.

46 Oyewùmi, *The Invention of Women,* 14–15.

47 Political somatics refers to somatic practice that is underpinned by
the intention to create social change. It is also called embodied social
justice; Staci K. Haines, *The Politics of Trauma: Somatics, Healing, and
Social Justice* (Berkeley, CA: North Atlantic Books, 2019).

48 Martha Eddy, *Mindful Movement: The Evolution of the Somatic Arts and
Conscious Action* (Bristol, UK: Intellect Books, 2016); Susan Raffo, *Liberated to the Bone: Histories. Bodies. Futures.* (Chico, CA: AK Press, 2022),
210–220.

49 Marya and Patel, *Inflamed,* 14–15.

50 Vandana Shiva, "Vandana Shiva on the Wisdom of Biodiversity,"
Atmos, March 10, 2022, https://atmos.earth/vandana-shiva-wisdom
-of-biodiversity/.

51 Shiva, "Vandana Shiva on the Wisdom of Biodiversity."

52 Blessings of the Forest home page, accessed July 10, 2023, https:
//blessingsoftheforest.org.

53 Raffo, *Liberated to the Bone,* 62.

54 Leanne Betasamosake Simpson, *As We Have Always Done* (Minneapolis: University of Minnesota Press, 2021), 3.

55 Yvonne Daniel, *Dancing Wisdom: Embodied Knowledge in Haitian Vodou, Cuban Yoruba, and Bahian Candomblé* (Chicago: University of Illinois Press, 2005).

56 Daniel, *Dancing Wisdom,* 276.

57 Daniel, *Dancing Wisdom,* 91.

58 I explore this topic more extensively in the chapter "Tending Grief Is Necessary within Social Movements."

59 Alchemical resilience is a core concept within the Resilience Toolkit. You can listen to Nkem speak more about it in the following podcast: https://podcasts.apple.com/ca/podcast/alchemical-resilience-with -nkem-ndefo/id885440301?i=1000497453662.

60 Rehearsing freedoms is a concept I first heard from Farzana Khan of Healing Justice London. It is inspired by scholar Ruth Wilson Gilmore's work on abolition—"abolition is life in rehearsal."

61 Nayyirah Waheed, *Salt.* (Nayyirah Waheed, 2013), 206.

62 Octavia Butler, *Parable of the Sower* (New York: Four Walls Eight Windows, 1993).

The Violence of the Void

1 This concept of *the Void* shares some parallels with the Anishinaabe tale of Wendigo about a cannibalistic monster. During the writing of this chapter, I came across the story in *Braiding Sweetgrass* by Robin Wall Kimmerer and felt it is an important story to acknowledge; Kimmerer, *Braiding Sweetgrass* (London: Penguin Books, 2020), 304–07.

2 Stephen Jenkinson, *Come of Age: The Case for Elderhood in a Time of Trouble* (Berkeley: North Atlantic Books, 2018), 231.

3 Adam Aronovich, *Healing from Healing* [blog and social media platform] accessed July 11, 2023, https://healingfromhealing.com. Aronovich speaks to the extractive and individualist dynamics within contemporary, Western wellness culture and the psychedelic space.

4 Jessica M. Yano, Kristie Yu, Gregory P. Donaldson, Gauri G. Shastri, Phoebe Ann, Liang Ma, Cathryn R. Nagler, Rustem F. Ismagilov, Sarkis K. Mazmanian, and Elaine Y. Hsiao, "Indigenous Bacteria from the Gut Microbiota Regulate Host Serotonin Biosynthesis," *Cell* 161, no. 2 (April 9, 2015): 264–276.

5 Kimmerer, *Braiding Sweetgrass*.

6 Jenkinson, *Come of Age*, 222–229.

7 Jenkinson, *Come of Age*, 222–229.

8 Jenkinson, *Come of Age*, 227.

9 Resmaa Menakem, *My Grandmother's Hands: Racialized Trauma and the Pathway to Mending Our Hearts and Bodies* (Las Vegas: Central Recovery Press, 2017), 59–63.

10 Sean McGlynn, "Violence and the Law in Medieval England," *History Today* 58, no. 4 (April 2008): 53.

11 Resmaa Menakem, "How Racism Began as White-on-White Violence," *Medium*, May 2, 2018, https://medium.com/@rmenakem/how-racism-began-as-white-on-white-violence-55b43ec1ccf3.

12 *Turtle Island* is a term used for North America by some Indigenous peoples.

13 Barbara Ehrenreich and Deirdre English, *Witches, Midwives and Nurses: A History of Women Healers* (New York: The Feminist Press, 2010), 5–6.

14 Brian Levack, *The Witch Hunt in Early Modern Europe* (Oxfordshire, UK: Routledge, 2006), 23.

15 The *commons* were communal lands that peasants could use under the feudal system to grow food, medicinal plants, and share space with others in the community. Silvia Federici, *Caliban and the Witch: Women, the Body and Primitive Accumulation* (New York: Autonomedia, 2004).

16 Ehrenreich and English, *Witches, Midwives and Nurses*, 3–8.

17 Federici, *Caliban and the Witch*, 42–45.

18 Federici, *Caliban and the Witch*, 84–90.

19 Federici, *Caliban and the Witch,* 164–165.

20 Nell Irvin Painter, *The History of White People* (New York: W. W. Norton & Company, 2018), 42.

21 Painter, *History of White People,* 40.

22 Elizabeth "Betita" Martinez, "What Is White Supremacy?," *Catalyst Project,* 2017, accessed July 11, 2023, www.pym.org/annual-sessions /wp-content/uploads/sites/7/2017/06/What_Is_White_Supremacy _Martinez.pdf.

23 Ira Berlin, "Race—The Power of an Illusion," *PBS,* 2003, accessed July 11, 2023, www.pbs.org/race/000_About/002_04-background-02-08.htm.

24 Berlin, "Race—The Power of an Illusion."

25 Frederique Marglin and Stephen Marglin, eds., *Decolonizing Knowledge: From Development to Dialogue* (New York: Oxford University Press, 1996).

26 Daniel, *Dancing Wisdom,* 57.

27 Madelanne Rust-D'Eye, "The Roots of White Supremacy Are in Our Bodies, Part 2: The Unthought Known," *Body Informed Leadership,* November 2017, www.bodyinformedleadership.org/resources/2017/11 /roots-white-supremacy-bodies-part-2-unthought-known.

28 White Awake [homepage], accessed July 19, 2023, https://whiteawake.org.

29 Aurora Levins Morales, *Medicine Stories: Essays for Radicals* (London: Duke University Press, 2019), 100–101.

Tending Grief Is Necessary within Social Movements

1 Staci K. Haines, "Safety, Belonging, and Dignity Are Identified as Core Needs for All Humans," in *The Politics of Trauma.*

2 Chris Crass, "How Can I Be Sexist? I'm an Anarchist!," in *Men Speak Out,* edited by Shira Tarrant (New York: Routledge, 2007), 276–284.

3 adrienne maree brown, "Octavia Tried to Tell Us," June 16, 2020, https://adriennemareebrown.net/2020/06/16/octavia-tried-to-tell-us/.

4 Emory Douglas, *Black Panther: The Revolutionary Art of Emory Douglas* (New York: Rizzoli, 2007).

5 Sanah Ahsan to author in some written feedback about this text, May 25, 2023.

6 Alexis Pauline Gumbs, China Martens, and Mai'a Williams, *Revolutionary Mothering: Love on the Front Lines* (New York: PM Press, 2016).

7 Deepa Iyer, Social Change Ecosystem Map, *Building Movement,* https://buildingmovement.org/our-work/movement-building/social-change-ecosystem-map/.

8 Rae Johnson, *Embodied Social Justice* (London: Routledge, 2018).

9 Johnson, *Embodied Social Justice,* 1.

10 Nick Montgomery and carla bergman, *Joyful Militancy: Building Thriving Resistance in Toxic Times* (Chico, CA: AK Press, 2017), 105–106.

11 Gustav Landauer, *Revolution and Other Writings: A Political Reader,* ed. Gabriel Kuhn (Oakland, CA: PM Press, 2010), 214.

12 Guilherme Fians, "Prefigurative Politics," *The Open Encyclopedia of Anthropology,* March 18, 2022, www.anthroencyclopedia.com/entry/prefigurative-politics.

13 Haines, *The Politics of Trauma,* 20–22.

14 Cindy Milstein, ed., *Rebellious Mourning: The Collective Work of Grief* (Chico, CA: AK Press, 2017).

15 Milstein, *Rebellious Mourning,* 4.

16 Devich-Cyril, "Grief Belongs in Social Movements. Can We Embrace It?"

17 It is worth noting that Extinction Rebellion has been inspired by the work of Joanna Macy and at times applies grief tending into their protests within the context of performance.

18 Montgomery and bergman, *Joyful Militancy,* 168–169.

19 Montgomery and bergman, *Joyful Militancy,* 175.

20 adrienne maree brown, *Pleasure Activism: The Politics of Feeling Good* (Chico, CA: AK Press, 2019).

21 *Britannica Online,* s.v. "cogito, ergo sum," accessed July 13, 2023, https: //www.britannica.com/topic/cogito-ergo-sum.

22 Thomas W. Merrill, "Masters and Possessors of Nature," *New Atlantis,* Winter 2008, www.thenewatlantis.com/publications/masters-and -possessors-of-nature.

23 Marya and Patel, *Inflamed.*

24 Silvia Federici, *Beyond the Periphery of the Skin: Rethinking, Remaking, and Reclaiming the Body in Contemporary Capitalism* (Oakland, CA: PM Press, 2020).

25 Federici, *Beyond the Periphery of the Skin,* 11–12.

26 Federici, *Beyond the Periphery of the Skin,* 12.

27 Hersey, *Rest Is Resistance,* 37–38.

28 Hersey, *Rest Is Resistance,* 37–38.

29 Hersey, *Rest Is Resistance,* 113–114.

30 "Prolonged Grief Disorder," American Psychiatric Association, accessed July 13, 2023, www.psychiatry.org/patients-families/prolonged-grief -disorder.

31 Malidoma Patrice Somé, *The Healing Wisdom of Africa: Finding Life Purpose through Nature, Ritual, and Community* (New York: Penguin Putnam, 1999), 219.

32 *Mental health oppression* is a term I was first exposed to within the Re-evaluation Counseling community.

33 Sanah Ahsan, "I'm a Psychologist—And I Believe We've Been Told Devastating Lies about Mental Health," *Guardian,* September 6, 2022, www.theguardian.com/commentisfree/2022/sep/06/psychologist -devastating-lies-mental-health-problems-politics.

34 Mary Watkins and Helene Shulman, *Towards Psychologies of Liberation* (London: Palgrave Macmillan, 2008), 26.

35 Marya and Patel, *Inflamed,* 62.

36 Marya and Patel, *Inflamed*, 93.

37 Marya and Patel, *Inflamed*, 62.

38 Somé, *The Healing Wisdom of Africa*, 131.

39 Somé, *The Healing Wisdom of Africa*, 129.

40 adrienne maree brown, *We Will Not Cancel Us: And Other Dreams of Transformative Justice* (Chico, CA: AK Press, 2020); Kai Cheng Thom, *I Hope We Choose Love* (Vancouver, Canada: Arsenal Pulp Press, 2019).

41 Prechtel, *The Smell of Rain on Dust*.

42 Charles Eisenstein, *Climate: A New Story* (Berkeley, CA: North Atlantic Books, 2018).

43 Haines, *The Politics of Trauma*, 21–25.

44 Haines, *The Politics of Trauma*, 25–26.

45 "Co-regulation," *Complex Trauma Resources,* accessed July 13, 2023, www.complextrauma.org/glossary/co-regulation/.

46 Lorde, *Sister Outsider,* 114–115.

A Conversation with Aisha from *misery* about Grief Work within the Club Context

1 miseryparty, Instagram, accessed July 19, 2023, www.instagram.com /miseryparty/?hl=en.

A Conversation with Zachi from Dopo about Abortion Companionship as Community Grief Work

1 To learn more about Dopo: www.wearedopo.com/about.

2 Department of Health and Social Care, "National Statistics: Abortion Statistics for England and Wales: 2019," June 11, 2020, www.gov.uk /government/statistics/abortion-statistics-for-england-and-wales-2019.

3 "Prolonged Grief Disorder."

4 Haroon Siddique, "New Bill Quietly Gives Powers to Remove British Citizenship without Notice," *Guardian,* November 17, 2021, https://www.theguardian.com/politics/2021/nov/17/new-bill-quietly-gives-powers-to-remove-british-citizenship-without-notice.

5 Federici, *Caliban and the Witch.*

How to Use These Grief Rituals

1 Haines, *The Politics of Trauma,* 23.

2 Francis Weller, *The Wild Edge of Sorrow: Rituals of Renewal and the Sacred Work of Grief* (Berkeley, CA: North Atlantic Books, 2015). Reprinted with permission from the publisher.

3 To learn more about how to incorporate vigils into protests, read Milstein, *Rebellious Mourning.*

4 This edition of Allied Media Conference took place in Detroit during 2019.

5 Prechtel, *The Smell of Rain on Dust.* Reprinted with permission of the publisher.

ABOUT THE AUTHOR

Camille Sapara Barton is a writer, artist, and embodied social justice facilitator. They have been tending grief since 2017 and have developed public resources, programs, and tools to cultivate the practice with others. Rooted in Black Feminism, ecology, and harm reduction, Camille is dedicated to creating networks of care and livable futures.

Based in Amsterdam, they designed and directed *Ecologies of Transformation* (2021 - 2023), a masters program exploring socially engaged art-making with a focus on creating change through the body into the world. Camille curates events and offers consultancy combining trauma informed practice, experiential learning, and their studies in political science. They love plants, music, and dancing.

ABOUT
NORTH ATLANTIC BOOKS

North Atlantic Books (NAB) is a 501(c)(3) nonprofit publisher committed to a bold exploration of the relationships between mind, body, spirit, culture, and nature. Founded in 1974, NAB aims to nurture a holistic view of the arts, sciences, humanities, and healing. To make a donation or to learn more about our books, authors, events, and newsletter, please visit www.northatlanticbooks.com.